Jenkins Fundamentals

Accelerate deliverables, manage builds, and automate
pipelines with Jenkins

Joseph Muli
Arnold Okoth

BIRMINGHAM - MUMBAI

Jenkins Fundamentals

Acquisitions Editor: Koushik Sen
Content Development Editors: Darren Patel, Neha Nair
Production Coordinator: Ratan Pote

First published: August 2018

Production reference: 1270818

Published by Packt Publishing Ltd.
Livery Place
35 Livery Street
Birmingham
B3 2PB, UK.

ISBN 978-1-78961-482-4

www.packtpub.com

`mapt.io`

Mapt is an online digital library that gives you full access to over 5,000 books and videos, as well as industry leading tools to help you plan your personal development and advance your career. For more information, please visit our website.

Why subscribe?

- Spend less time learning and more time coding with practical eBooks and Videos from over 4,000 industry professionals

- Improve your learning with Skill Plans built especially for you

- Get a free eBook or video every month

- Mapt is fully searchable

- Copy and paste, print, and bookmark content

PacktPub.com

Did you know that Packt offers eBook versions of every book published, with PDF and ePub files available? You can upgrade to the eBook version at `www.PacktPub.com` and as a print book customer, you are entitled to a discount on the eBook copy. Get in touch with us at `service@packtpub.com` for more details.

At `www.PacktPub.com`, you can also read a collection of free technical articles, sign up for a range of free newsletters, and receive exclusive discounts and offers on Packt books and eBooks.

Contributors

About the Authors

Joseph Muli loves programming, writing, teaching, gaming, and traveling. He's currently working as a software engineer at Andela and Fathom, specializing in DevOps and Site Reliability. Previously, he worked as a software engineer and technical mentor at Moringa School.

Arnold Okoth is a software developer at Andela with three years' experience of extensive development and system operations. He has worked with Python, Jenkins, Docker, AWS, and Bash. Arnold has gained numerous certifications in the fields of networking, application security, and cloud computing from industry-leading vendors, such as Amazon, Cisco, and IBM. During his downtime, Arnold enjoys watching sports – mainly football and basketball.

Packt is Searching for Authors Like You

If you're interested in becoming an author for Packt, please visit `authors.packtpub.com` and apply today. We have worked with thousands of developers and tech professionals, just like you, to help them share their insight with the global tech community. You can make a general application, apply for a specific hot topic that we are recruiting an author for, or submit your own idea.

Table of Contents

Preface

Jenkins is a scalable and highly efficient open source automation server that runs an unparalleled plugin ecosystem. It is written in Java and uses plugins designed for continuous integration, deployment, and automation purposes.

Developing and testing application software can be a very expensive and time-consuming process. Individuals and enterprises are continuously looking to automate unit testing and workflows, and merge working copies of files with a mainline. Jenkins allows users to automate tasks related to scheduling, modifying code, and using triggers. It uses functions and plugins to automate the workflow and move from the continuous integration of working code copies toward continuous delivery, where the code is automatically built, tested, and deployed for production release.

This book balances theory and exercises, and contains multiple open-ended activities that use real-life business scenarios for you to practice and apply your newly acquired skills in a highly relevant context. We have included over 30 practical activities and exercises across 18 topics to reinforce your learning. After completing this book, you will be able to:

- Set up and deploy a Jenkins server across different platforms via Docker
- Design development workflows that enable continuous integration and then easily integrate with Jenkins
- Explore community plugins and use them to extend core Jenkins functionality
- Set up a freestyle project as well as a view to manage your projects
- Understand source control and pipelines, and build parameters in the context of Git and Jenkins
- Configure general-purpose freestyle projects, or use more formal pipeline-driven implementation

Who this book is for

This book is aimed at new developers and operations personnel looking to set up continuous integration and delivery pipelines specifically with Jenkins. You should have basic programming experience and a working knowledge of test-driven development, experience of using the Bash command-line interface and of managing virtual machines using tools such as Vagrant and Virtualbox, as well as a basic knowledge of Docker images and containers.

What this book covers

Chapter 1, *Installing and Setting up Jenkins*, covers the installing and setup of Jenkins. We will talk about various features of the Jenkins dashboard and analyze how Jenkins handles user management and security.

Chapter 2, *Administering Jenkins*, discusses the need for plugin management in Jenkins and covers the various plugin types available. We will understand how to update and upgrade Jenkins to newer versions and also configure Jenkins for production.

Chapter 3, *Jenkins Views and Freestyle Projects*, explains how to setup freestyle projects and views to manage projects. We will identify what it takes to make build environments more convenient and efficient through views.

Chapter 4, *Parameterized and Up/Downstream Project*, covers the various build parameters and their importance, and explains how they can be accessed. We will also learn how to create upstream and downstream projects and demonstrate the importance of build triggers.

Chapter 5, *Jenkins Pipelines*, demonstrates how to identify and integrate Git workflows that enable CI and use the declarative Jenkins pipeline. We will also talk about the role of the Jenkinsfile in a Jenkins pipeline.

Chapter 6, *Distributed Builds on Jenkins*, discusses how to connect agents to your Jenkins master and access them securely. We will also learn how to run freestyle and pipeline projects on our agents.

To get the most out of this book

You will require a computer system with at least an Intel Core i5 processor, 4 GB RAM, and 35 GB of storage space operating on a Windows 7 or higher operating system. Along with this, you would require the following software:

1. Browser: Google Chrome or Mozilla Firefox (latest updates installed)
2. Docker
3. Git
4. Python
5. Blue Ocean

Download the example code files

You can download the example code files for this book from your account at `www.packtpub.com`. If you purchased this book elsewhere, you can visit `www.packtpub.com/support` and register to have the files emailed directly to you.

You can download the code files by following these steps:

1. Log in or register at `www.packtpub.com`.
2. Select the **SUPPORT** tab.
3. Click on **Code Downloads & Errata**.
4. Enter the name of the book in the **Search** box and follow the onscreen instructions.

Once the file is downloaded, please make sure that you unzip or extract the folder using the latest version of:

- WinRAR/7-Zip for Windows
- Zipeg/iZip/UnRarX for Mac
- 7-Zip/PeaZip for Linux

The code bundle for the book is also hosted on GitHub at `https://github.com/TrainingByPackt/Beginning-Jenkins`. In case there's an update to the code, it will be updated on the existing GitHub repository.

We also have other code bundles from our rich catalog of books and videos available at `https://github.com/PacktPublishing/`. Check them out!

Conventions used

There are a number of text conventions used throughout this book.

`CodeInText`: Indicates code words in text, database table names, folder names, filenames, file extensions, pathnames, dummy URLs, user input, and Twitter handles. Here is an example: "Mount the downloaded `WebStorm-10*.dmg` disk image file as another disk in your system."

A block of code is set as follows:

```
html, body, #map {
  height: 100%;
  margin: 0;
  padding: 0
}
```

When we wish to draw your attention to a particular part of a code block, the relevant lines or items are set in bold:

```
[default]
exten => s,1,Dial(Zap/1|30)
exten => s,2,Voicemail(u100)
exten => s,102,Voicemail(b100)
exten => i,1,Voicemail(s0)
```

Any command-line input or output is written as follows:

```
$ mkdir css
$ cd css
```

Bold: Indicates a new term, an important word, or words that you see onscreen. For example, words in menus or dialog boxes appear in the text like this. Here is an example: "Select **System info** from the **Administration** panel."

 Warnings or important notes appear like this.

 Tips and tricks appear like this.

Get in touch

Feedback from our readers is always welcome.

General feedback: Email `feedback@packtpub.com` and mention the book title in the subject of your message. If you have questions about any aspect of this book, please email us at `questions@packtpub.com`.

Errata: Although we have taken every care to ensure the accuracy of our content, mistakes do happen. If you have found a mistake in this book, we would be grateful if you would report this to us. Please visit `www.packtpub.com/submit-errata`, selecting your book, clicking on the Errata Submission Form link, and entering the details.

Piracy: If you come across any illegal copies of our works in any form on the Internet, we would be grateful if you would provide us with the location address or website name. Please contact us at `copyright@packtpub.com` with a link to the material.

If you are interested in becoming an author: If there is a topic that you have expertise in and you are interested in either writing or contributing to a book, please visit `authors.packtpub.com`.

Reviews

Please leave a review. Once you have read and used this book, why not leave a review on the site that you purchased it from? Potential readers can then see and use your unbiased opinion to make purchase decisions, we at Packt can understand what you think about our products, and our authors can see your feedback on their book. Thank you!

For more information about Packt, please visit `packtpub.com`.

Installing and Setting up Jenkins

1

This chapter will cover Continuous Delivery, how the process impacts the software development life cycle, and how Jenkins is set up to enforce the process. We shall also get to explore a real-world Continuous Delivery pipeline and all the stages and services involved.

Let's begin the chapter with a glance at Continuous Delivery and the various enablers, before understanding why and how Jenkins is involved in the process.

By the end of this chapter, you will be able to:

- Explain Continuous Delivery and its impacts on a development life cycle
- Identify Continuous Delivery enablers
- Set up and install Jenkins
- Describe the Jenkins dashboard
- Set up prerequisite configurations

Continuous Delivery

What is Continuous Delivery?

Continuous Delivery is the ability to get changes and updates of all types to end users or production as safely and as quickly as possible. The goal should always be easy deployment on demand, whether of a simple **Hello World** application or a large distributed or embedded system. This includes providing resources, such as processing power at runtime.

Before we proceed, let's discuss a few important terms:

- **Continuous Delivery**–involves a manual trigger to production.
- **Continuous Deployment**–involves automatic releases to production.
- **Continuous Integration**– is usually the initial part of both Continuous Delivery and Deployment, involving the testing and building of any new or updated source code.

 If the process is slow and painful, you're doing something wrong.

As discussed above, Continuous Delivery, also known as **CD**, is a process that enables the delivery of the final product in a development cycle. Companies such as Amazon, Walmart, Target, and Facebook all use CD.

Getting software to users is often very slow, painful, and costly. CD innovates the process through the following:

- **Minimal release management:** Developers are able to deploy changes, bug fixes, and feedback implementation to any desired environment painlessly and seamlessly.
- **Feedback loops are faster:** Feedback from end users or QA is deployed in the most efficient way by tools, without human intervention.
- **Work with market demand:** With continuous delivery, the adoption of a change, either in business strategy or a shift in the market, can be incorporated in the easiest way possible.
- **Testing and QA made easier:** Developers can finally update changes from testing and QA faster.

How and Where is Jenkins Involved?

Jenkins is one of the leading open source automation servers, providing countless plugins to support the building, deployment, and automation of any project. Jenkins can almost be described as a CI/CD framework, because much of the logic needed to automate a project is achieved through plugins. This gives the server a greater advantage over other CI/CD servers, because any new language, framework, or tool can be easily set up on Jenkins through these plugins. Did you know that plugins are built by the vast developer community?

Jenkins also provides an effective separation of concerns for everyone involved in the software's life cycle. For instance, developers get to focus on their code; the quality assurance team is solely responsible for quality measures because testing is automated through Jenkins.

In a nutshell, Jenkins has the following advantages over software development:

- It is open source and completely free.
- Issues with tests and builds are detected easily and reported almost immediately.
- Jenkins is platform independent, available on Windows, macOS, and Linux.
- It is easily configurable and customizable for any project.

Let's have a look at the basic workflow of a Continuous Delivery pipeline with Jenkins, and what would be involved in the process. Take a look at these steps:

 The following is also a real-world Continuous Delivery pipeline implementation.

1. The first step is making sure your code is up to date with **Origin**, the code base hosted on GitHub.
2. Branch out and make the required changes.
    - Check out to your branch and make the necessary changes; don't forget your tests.
    - Run your tests; are they passing? If yes, then proceed ahead.
3. Confirm whether your branch is up to date with Origin.
4. Commit and push your changes to Origin. This is where Jenkins takes over.
5. Jenkins will build any new update to the GitHub repository.
6. If the test runs pass, an automatic build will be triggered by Jenkins.

Here is a simple diagram describing the steps above and Continuous Delivery in general:

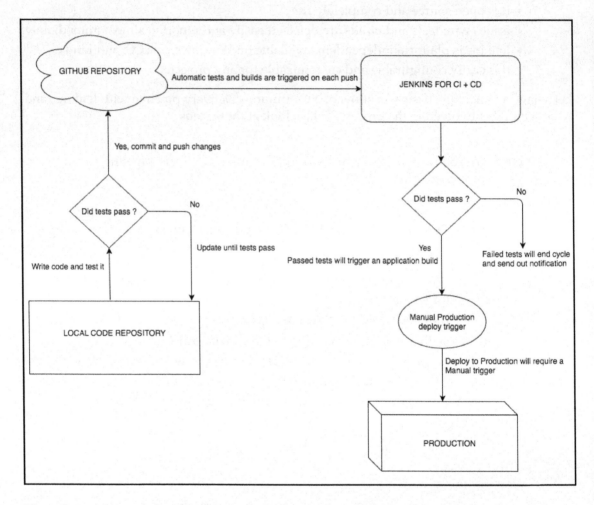

Now that we have defined Jenkins' role in Continuous Delivery, let's get started on our pipeline, but first let's set up Jenkins.

Installing Jenkins

There are various ways to install and run Jenkins. You can install Jenkins using a WAR (Web Application Archive) file available for Windows. However, we shall be looking at a Jenkins installation through Docker, because it's cross-platform and super easy to set up.

Before we set up the server, let's reflect on some efficiency notes on setting up Jenkins:

- Jenkins is platform independent, available on Windows, macOS, and Linux:

  Jenkins is supported on Windows and Unix. Better yet, we will be using Docker, which means the commands we will run will be similar, with slight syntax differences on different platforms.

- Jenkins is easily configurable, and customizable to any project:

  Before we even set up the server, we already know we can customize Jenkins to run any of the projects we come up with.

- Jenkins has a rich plugin system:

  Jenkins supports a vast number of plugins, some of which we shall be setting up when installing the server.

Setting up Jenkins

Now, we'll set up a Jenkins host on your computer. The following steps will show you how to do this. Pay attention to the notes and tips throughout the book.

1. Open Git Bash and run the docker command to verify that the service is running. Be sure to start Docker if the service is not running.

Take a look at this screenshot:

```
→ ~ docker

Usage:  docker COMMAND

A self-sufficient runtime for containers

Options:
      --config string      Location of client config files (default "/Users/josephmuli/.docker")
  -D, --debug              Enable debug mode
  -H, --host list          Daemon socket(s) to connect to
  -l, --log-level string   Set the logging level ("debug"|"info"|"warn"|"error"|"fatal") (default "info")
      --tls                Use TLS; implied by --tlsverify
      --tlscacert string   Trust certs signed only by this CA (default "/Users/josephmuli/.docker/ca.pem")
      --tlscert string     Path to TLS certificate file (default "/Users/josephmuli/.docker/cert.pem")
      --tlskey string      Path to TLS key file (default "/Users/josephmuli/.docker/key.pem")
      --tlsverify          Use TLS and verify the remote
  -v, --version            Print version information and quit

Management Commands:
  checkpoint  Manage checkpoints
  config      Manage Docker configs
  container   Manage containers
  image       Manage images
  network     Manage networks
  node        Manage Swarm nodes
  plugin      Manage plugins
  secret      Manage Docker secrets
  service     Manage services
```

2. On Git Bash, run the following command, shown in this screenshot:

```
→ ~ docker run ^
-u root ^
– rm ^
-d ^
-p 8080:8080 ^
-v jenkins-data:/var/jenkins_home ^
-v /var/run/docker.sock:/var/run/docker.sock ^
jenkinsci/blueocean
```

The preceding command pulls the Jenkins image and runs Jenkins in the Docker container built from the image. The syntax is quite similar on all platforms (Windows, Linux, Mac), with very few differences.

The command we just ran will attempt to run the **Jenkinsci** image. If not found locally, the image will be pulled from Docker Hub.

Take a look at this table of the commands we would be using:

Command	Explanation
`docker run`	The Docker command to run our container
`-u root`	The user we want to run our container as
`--rm (optional)`	Automatically removes the container when it's shut down or when you quit Jenkins
`-d (optional)`	Runs our container in the background
`-p 8080:8080`	Maps our computer's port to the container's port, in that order
`-v jenkins-data:/var/jenkins_home (optional)`	Maps the `jenkins_home` container directory to a volume with the name `jenkins-data`.
`-v /var/run/docker.sock:/var/run/docker.sock (optional)`	Allows the container to communicate with the Docker daemon, when instantiating new containers
`jenkinsci/blueocean`	The Jenkins image

3. On completion, we should have the following results:

```
➜ ~ docker run \
-u root \
--rm \
-d \
-p 8080:8080 \
-p 50000:50000 \
-v jenkins-data:/var/jenkins_home \
-v /var/run/docker.sock:/var/run/docker.sock \
jenkinsci/blueocean
Unable to find image 'jenkinsci/blueocean:latest' locally
latest: Pulling from jenkinsci/blueocean
ff3a5c916c92: Pull complete
5de5f69f42d7: Pull complete
fd869c8b9b59: Pull complete
97056f636d5a: Pull complete
b8735f69f698: Pull complete
c927d6aa54da: Pull complete
569dbe3bfcf5: Pull complete
28a1b4b2f3f2: Pull complete
bc956c71de07: Pull complete
bbf22d011438: Pull complete
f3870509cbc0: Pull complete
60946888fa2b: Pull complete
1fa1da5a0b03: Pull complete
7f68842a03b5: Pull complete
4860712e0614: Pull complete
Digest: sha256:505d814c7bc5215112343fff45175b6dd21b510b19fe9b900b83038ccbfeea2e
Status: Downloaded newer image for jenkinsci/blueocean:latest
b3672a0834dc16494ba0bfc765b1f22b75e8df81b34d86c6335fe2a52078b8e6
➜ ~
```

Go to `http://localhost:8080` to view the following output:

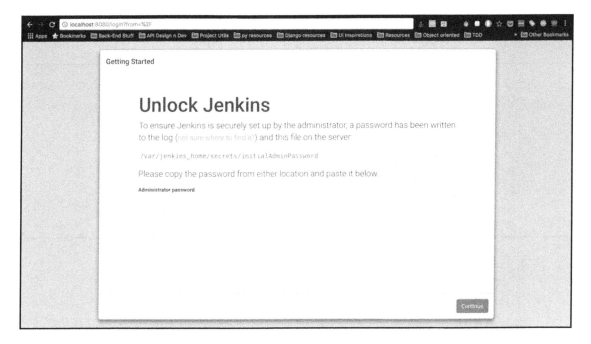

A closer look at the message shows us how Jenkins prioritizes security above anything else. This also proves to be a crucial advantage of having a system admin or DevOps engineer who would be responsible for system setup, upgrades, general maintenance, and operations.

This step proves that every engineering team needs to limit access to production and utility software, which is a highly encouraged practice, enabling processes such as audits and, of course, reducing human error on production servers. Take a look at this screenshot.

To ensure Jenkins is securely set up by the administrator, a password has been written to the log (not sure where to find it?) and this file on the server:

```
/var/jenkins_home/secrets/initialAdminPassword
```

Please copy the password from either location and paste it below.

Administrator password

4. Get the password from the **container logs** by first identifying the **docker container ID**.

5. Run the `docker ps command`. Take a look at this screenshot:

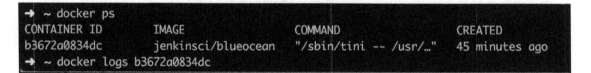

```
➜  ~ docker ps
CONTAINER ID        IMAGE              COMMAND             CREATED
b3672a0834dc        jenkinsci/blueocean  "/sbin/tini -- /usr/…"  45 minutes ago
➜  ~ docker logs b3672a0834dc
```

This will identify all of the running containers. Our Jenkins container will have `jenkinsci/blueocean` as the image name.

6. Run `docker logs <add container id here>` to get the logs. The password will be listed within the asterisk characters from the Jenkins console log output. Take a look at this screenshot:

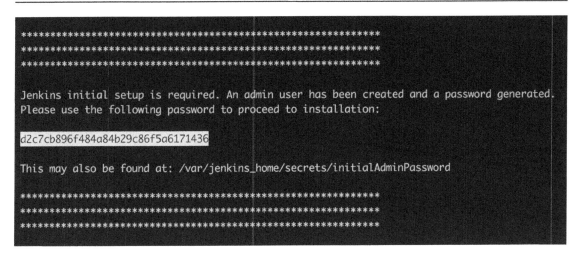

```
**********************************************************
**********************************************************
**********************************************************

Jenkins initial setup is required. An admin user has been created and a password generated.
Please use the following password to proceed to installation:

d2c7cb896f484a84b29c86f5a6171436

This may also be found at: /var/jenkins_home/secrets/initialAdminPassword

**********************************************************
**********************************************************
**********************************************************
```

7. Copy the password and paste it on to the browser prompt; we are almost ready.

> If you are asked for a username, use `root`. Make sure to save
> your password somewhere secure, as you may need it if you quit Jenkins.

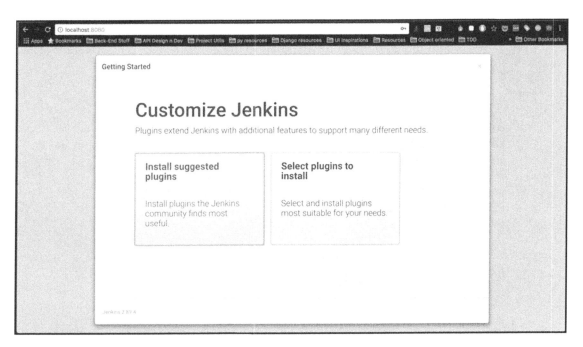

8. Select **Install Suggested plugins**. The download speed will vary depending on your internet speed. Take a look at this screenshot:

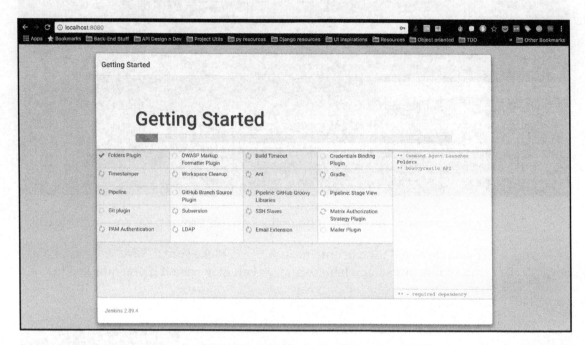

We'll add more later when we look into the best practices when designing a Continuous Delivery pipeline.

9. After the plugin setup is complete, Jenkins will prompt you to create an administrator user. Fill in the details in the respective fields and click on **Save** and **Finish**. Take a look at this screenshot:

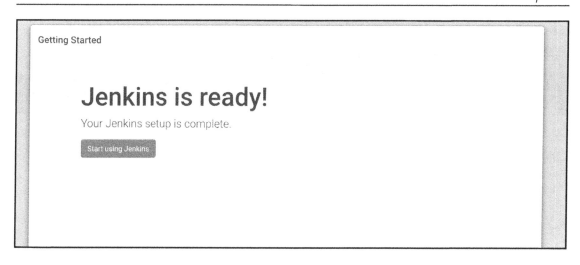

Getting Started

Jenkins is ready!

Your Jenkins setup is complete.

Start using Jenkins

From this point on, Jenkins can only be accessed through valid credentials.

The Jenkins Dashboard

The Jenkins dashboard is the central point of all operations in our pipelines and projects. Any and all operations are coordinated from this point.

From the dashboard, we are able to achieve operations not limited to the following:

- Project and pipeline management
- Access control
- Data and resource management

Once the Jenkins setup is complete, click on **Start using Jenkins** on the landing screen, and let's get started.

If the page still shows Jenkins is almost ready, click on **Restart**. If the page doesn't restart or update after a minute, reload your web page manually.

If required to log in, use the credentials we just created on the UI, and you should be good to go. Take a look at this screenshot:

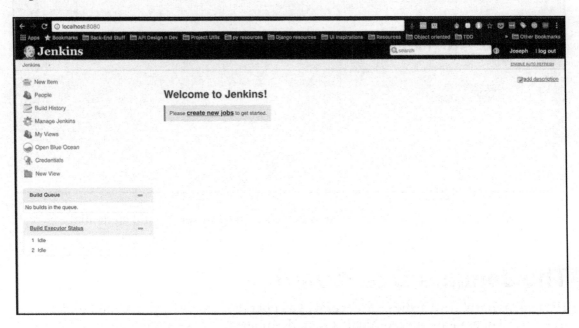

At first glance, we have a few options listed there. When you first log into Jenkins and you don't have any jobs or builds, the above will be the message displayed. In the top-right corner, there is an option to add a description. This is where you would add typical information about the server and guide, for example, some company info, as shown in the following screenshot:

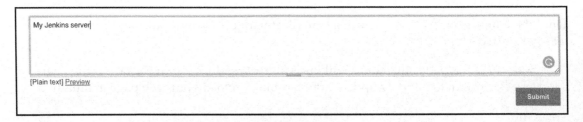

In the top-right corner, there's a drop-down linked to your username. There are a few items to note here; they are as follows:

- **Builds:** Option to view all pipeline builds.
- **Configure:** Add a new project or Job.

- **User Views:** Display custom user views.
- **Credentials:** Display credentials, if authorized.

The drop-down panel gives us a few items to note too. Take a look at this screenshot:

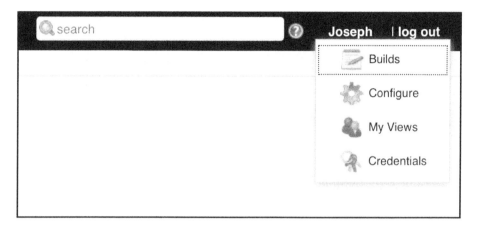

The drop-down panel lists the following:

Selection	Explanation
New Item	Allows the user to create a new item, which could be a project, pipeline, and so on.
People	Lists all the users available.
Build History	Shows all builds.
Manage Jenkins	Lists all configurations related to the Jenkins server.
My Views	Lists all custom user views.
Credentials	Lists all of the user and server credentials available.
New View	Allows you to create a new view.

 Some of the options will change when access is controlled for different users.

In the bottom-right corner, there's a **REST API** button, with some information on how to interact with the Jenkins API. Take a look at this screenshot:

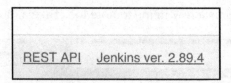

Now take a look at this screenshot:

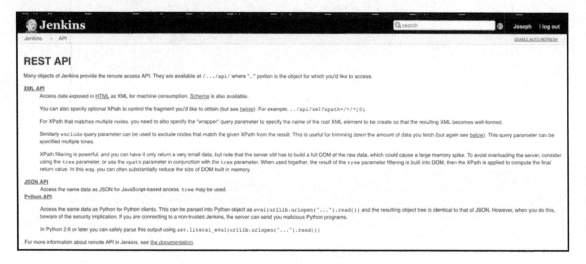

We will learn more about this when designing and building a pipeline, as there are some instances where you would be required to programmatically interact with Jenkins or run some scripts to get metrics or artifacts.

 It is important to understand the dashboard as much as possible, so as to know where you would get and/or use a particular service. For now, we will solely focus on General Management and the setup of Jenkins, but as we progress, we will delve deeper into the service, giving us more information regarding the handling operations in Jenkins.

User Management

User Management describes the ability of administrators or super users to control access to resources and services, such as creating, stopping, or deleting Jenkins' pipelines.

User management is a core security essential and one of the enablers of security audits. Controlled access, as we discussed earlier, limits human error to production servers, for example, someone accidentally deleting a host or, in this case, a build and eventually deploying a buggy service, causing downtime.

User Management

Now we'll analyze how Jenkins handles user management and security.

1. Open **Manage Jenkins** and then select the **Configure Global Security** settings as follows. Take a look at this screenshot:

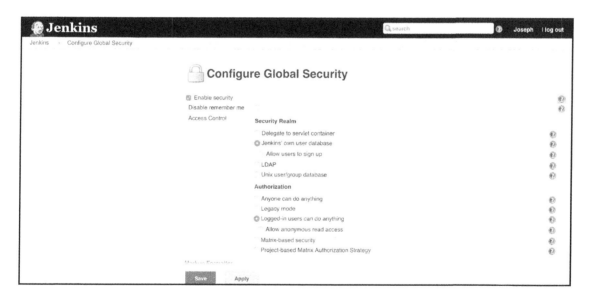

By default, we should have security enabled and the Security Realm as **Jenkins' own user database**. Authorization is also set to the default, allowing all users to do anything when logged in. While this might be OK if only one user exists, having more users can be hazardous if no control exists.

Let's have a look at what some of the options under **Authorization** perform:

- **Matrix-based security**: Allows the admin to grant permissions in groups, divided into contexts. Take a look at this screenshot:

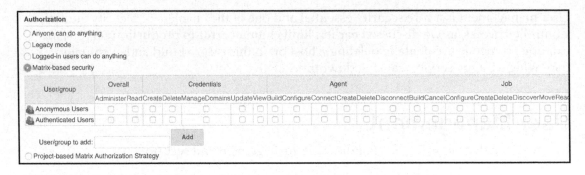

- **Legacy mode**: Grants the administrator all rights, and limits everyone else to read-only access.

- **Project-based Matrix Authorization Strategy**: Gives control over group permissions per project.

2. Select **Matrix-based security**, and add a new user to your current account.

 If you added admin, when you signed up, type in `admin` as follows.

3. Click on **Add**, and your user first and last names should appear on the list.
4. Select all checkboxes for the administrator, and then select **Apply** and save the changes. Take a look at this screenshot:

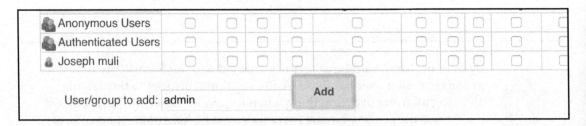

Activity: User Management and Security

Scenario

You have been asked to create two user accounts: an Ops engineer and a developer account. Both users should have different access levels from the administrator account. The Ops engineer will only not be able to do the following:

- Administer
- Create credentials
- View credentials
- Delete credentials
- Update credentials

The developer will only be able to have overall **Read** permissions.

Aim

To create users with different access permissions and resource controls.

Steps for Completion

1. Select the **Manage Jenkins** option from the configuration panel. Take a look at this screenshot:

2. Select the **Manage Users** option. Take a look at this screenshot:

Manage Old Data
Scrub configuration files to remove remnants from old plugins and earl

Manage Users
Create/delete/modify users that can log in to this Jenkins

Prepare for Shutdown
Stops executing new builds, so that the system can be eventually shut

3. Select the **Create User** option on the left-hand side navigation bar. Take a look at this screenshot:

Back to Dashboard

Manage Jenkins

Create User

4. Go to the **Configure Global Security** option. Take a look at this screenshot:

Configure Global Security
Secure Jenkins; define who is allowed to access/use the system.

5. Under **Authorization**, select **Matrix-based security**.

6. Add the new users.

7. Update the users' permissions as shown in the following screenshot:

We have successfully created two user accounts: an ops engineer account and a developer account with different access permissions and resource controls.

Summary

In this chapter, we have differentiated between Continuous Integration, Delivery, and Deployment processes and included how each is equally important in achieving an effective pipeline. We have identified efficiency points on setting up a Jenkins server on different platforms, and also set up a server on Docker. Lastly, we have gained a high-level understanding of user management and access control.

In the following chapters, we shall demonstrate the effect access control has on Jenkins resources through plugin management and updates and upgrades to Jenkins and its resources. In most, if not all cases, only a user with the correct set of privileges has the ability to run and manage these services, as we shall find out.

Administering Jenkins 2

In the previous chapter, we covered a few basic steps on getting started with Jenkins. From that knowledge, we were able to get conversant with the dashboard, set up user accounts with secure and limited access, and have our server running locally on Docker. We are almost ready to do some build magic.

We can confidently identify the role of Jenkins, not only in a continuous delivery pipeline but also in the software development life cycle. This is a great advantage, allowing us to think of more ways to automate workflows, making development easier and more fun.

This chapter will cover knowledge on plugins and production readiness, as we build on our pipeline and how the process enables delivery. We will also demonstrate how Jenkins is set up to enforce this process.

By the end of this chapter, you will be able to:

- Explain the need for plugin management in Jenkins
- Implement various plugin types to enhance Jenkins functionality
- Implement the necessary tools and practices for a production-like server
- Upgrade Jenkins to stable versions when required

Plugin Management

First, let's take a few minutes and assess what we want to achieve. In the previous chapter, we had a slight glance at **Continuous Integration (CI)**. To quickly recap this, CI is the process of continuously merging code on a shared repository, followed by automated testing and builds. We also identified the process as the first stage in any Continuous Delivery or Deployment pipeline.

As we build on our Continuous Delivery pipeline, we'll start with a simple CI build. This is to basically help us get used to the process. Moreover, a number of very crucial principles and guides will be covered, giving us a dynamic view of CI pipelines and builds. This knowledge is applicable to other tools and processes, too.

Here's a quick glance at what we want to achieve:

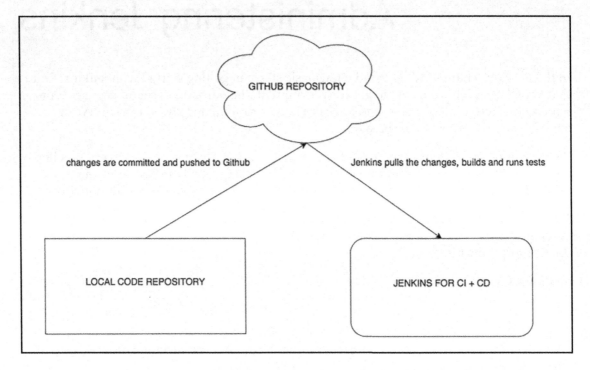

The workflow basically involves the following:

1. When code is pushed to GitHub, however little, we can pull the codebase from Jenkins, run the tests, and if they pass, the changes can be merged if a pull request was raised. If they fail, Jenkins will notify us through the notification channels that have been defined. To achieve this, we would normally require a few tools and services.
2. Use of Git, which is a tool that helps version code collaboratively. If you are running Git Bash, run the following command to confirm that Git is running as expected:

```
➜  ~ git
usage: git [--version] [--help] [-C <path>] [-c name=value]
           [--exec-path[=<path>]] [--html-path] [--man-path] [--info-path]
           [-p | --paginate | --no-pager] [--no-replace-objects] [--bare]
           [--git-dir=<path>] [--work-tree=<path>] [--namespace=<name>]
           <command> [<args>]

These are common Git commands used in various situations:
```

3. We also need Jenkins plugins. Plugins are resources that enable us to utilize
   services, including third-party applications, and achieve more operations on
   Jenkins. We shall identify and demonstrate the different types of plugins in the
   next section.

First, let's prepare Jenkins and come back to this at a later stage.

Plugin management is a skill and a requirement that's crucial for anyone willing to unleash
Jenkins' full potential. On its own, the Jenkins server will not always fit everyone's
requirements. In fact, with all the new tools being released almost weekly, Jenkins will
probably be the last CI/CD server you will think of.

With plugins, Jenkins is able to become resourceful and efficient, still giving anyone a
chance to add custom plugins to fit any project requirement. Plugins can achieve a lot
regarding what people want to set up, for example:

- Do you want to send a notification after every build? There's a plugin for that.
- Most, if not all programming languages have supporting plugins for
  building and running.

We have recently gone through a few administrative tools and processes on Jenkins. While
we're still on that subject, you may have noticed a few third-party integrations on your
Jenkins server, for example:

Under **Configure System** through **Manage Jenkins**, you will notice the following:

Take a look at this screenshot:

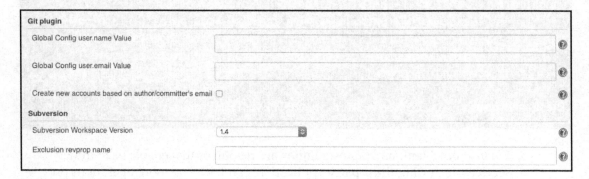

There are a few more listed that aren't in the preceding screenshots, and you may have noticed that while we installed the server, there was an option to set up these plugins.

In most cases, when working with Jenkins, you will want to run an operation that is not readily available on Jenkins by default. What would you do then?

Plugins can modify Jenkins in multiple and extensible ways. By default, Jenkins has limited features that may not support a lot of the tools that are released almost weekly, but with a very active community, we are able to get support through plugins. Before we identify the different kinds of plugins available and those we need for our pipelines, let's go over a few principles of working with plugins. Keep in mind to only set up what you need.

Principles of Plugin Usage

Plugins in the Jenkins environment are used to improve the functionality and meet user requirements. Here are a few key points to remember:

- Always read through a plugin's documentation and guide to understand whether it achieves your intended goals.
- Before installing, check the usage statistics and update frequency.
- Will it work with your Jenkins server version?
- Understanding how it works will have a great impact on how much help the tool provides, allowing you to maximize the potential.

Let's go through and recognize a few plugin types as we prepare to enforce our Jenkins server.

Feel free to follow through the Official Plugin Index at `https://plugins.jenkins.io/`.

Administration Plugins

These plugins are related but not limited to the following:

Administration plugins will help customize access control and the overall management of the host.

- **Service authentication**: Introduction of new ways to access the host and its services, for example, LDAP.
- **Audit trail and general security**: Follow up on who did what; limit access to services and various operations
- **Node and job-related management**: Allows a variety of node-related operations, including the support of multiple operating system requirements.

User Interface (UI) Plugins

UI plugins that help customize the Jenkins UI may provide the following:

- Customizing the view tabs, menu, and dropdowns
- Formatting text, and even images
- Email templates

Source Code Management (SCM) Plugins

SCM plugins are what help integrate version control services. They provide the following:

- Allow Jenkins to run version control systems such as Git, Mercurial, and SCM.
- Allow Jenkins to pull code from version control hosts, such as GitHub, Bitbucket, GitLab, and so on.
- Authenticate Jenkins to pull from both private and public version control hosts.

The points we have listed here are not the full potential of the plugin types. The possibilities are infinite.

Build Management Plugins

Build Management are plugins that are involved in any build step. A point to consider here is that if you ever need a feature or process done that is not readily available on Jenkins, be sure to check the plugin index. Consider the following:

- Allow Jenkins to trigger notifications on build failure or pass
- Manage build artifacts
- Trigger deploys or other custom build steps

Now let's get back to our server and walk through how to work with plugins.

Setting up Jenkins with Plugins

Now, we'll set up a Jenkins host on your computer. Click on **Manage Jenkins** and select **Manage Plugins**. Take a look at this screenshot:

Reload Configuration from Disk
Discard all the loaded data in memory and reload everything from file system. Usefu

Manage Plugins
Add, remove, disable or enable plugins that can extend the functionality of Jenkins.

System Information
Displays various environmental information to assist trouble-shooting.

The next page displays the Plugin Management dashboard. Notice that a couple are the ones that we installed while setting up the Jenkins server:

The four tabs at the top give us options to do the following:

- **Updates**: Check for updates on currently installed plugins.
- **Available**: Check for available plugins directly from the plugin index. This means that you don't have to open this on a new browser tab, unless you are handling a critical operation on Jenkins.
- **Installed**: All currently installed plugins, both pre-and post-installation of the plugins.
- **Advanced**: The final tab allows us to add a custom plugin to Jenkins.

Sometimes, keeping up to date with the newest versions is not always the best idea. Always seek more information on the stable releases and work with those, unless they become outdated.

Installing a Sample Plugin

Now, we'll install a sample plugin for `InternetMeme`.

1. Open the **Plugin Manager** page and head to the **Available** tab, as follows:

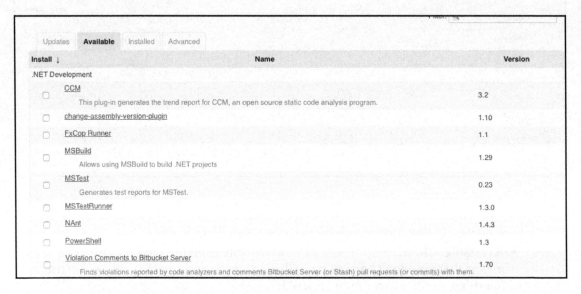

2. Search for **InternetMeme** on the **Filter** tab, and the results should be as follows:

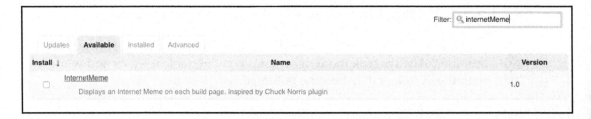

Before we install the plugin, let's understand what it's all about, how to use it, and the statistics behind the plugin. Open the following link: `https://plugins.jenkins.io/internetmeme`.

There are some key items to notice:

- Number of installs and last release date. Take a look at this screenshot:

Installs: 366
GitHub →
Last released: 4 years ago

- Download instructions and usage. Take a look at this screenshot:

Download & Installation
You can download it directly from the Plugins Update Center.

Usage
1. Go to the job configuration page and check the "Activate Internet Meme" checkbox in the "Post Build Actions" dropdown
2. Post build run, a random meme image is displayed on the build page.

This is all we need for now, so let's go back to our server and set this up.

3. Back on the **Plugin Manager** page, select the checkbox and click on **Download now and install after restart**. Take a look at this screenshot:

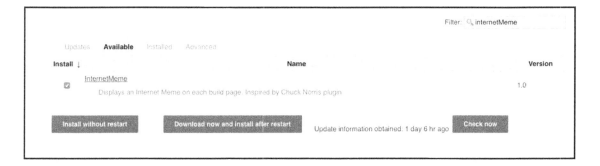

Something to note here is that we are currently not running any jobs on our server, so it's OK to restart the host.

Do not do this on a production server, as you might interfere with someone else's build or, more than likely, a scheduled job.

4. Jenkins will still ask you to verify whether you want to restart after installation, when no jobs are running after this. Take a look at this screenshot:

Installing Plugins/Upgrades

Preparation
- Checking internet connectivity
- Checking update center connectivity

Windows Slaves   ● Pending

External Monitor Job Type   ● Pending

InternetMeme   ● Pending

Go back to the top page
(you can start using the installed plugins right away)

☐ Restart Jenkins when installation is complete and no jobs are running

---

You may notice more plugins installing when we only chose one. Don't be alarmed —some plugins may depend on services that are not readily available on your server.

5. Select **Restart Jenkins when installation is complete and no jobs are running**. This is, however, the option you would take if you are not aware of who is currently running a job. The result should be as follows:

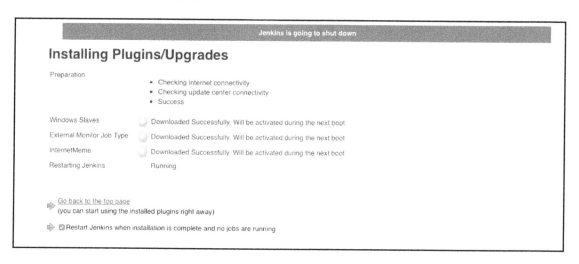

If everything works as anticipated, you should be back on the main dashboard page. Sometimes, the connection may be slow, and to fix this, after the plugins have been successfully installed, we'll need to perform a safe restart. On the navigation bar, update the URL to match the following:

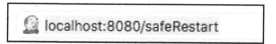

6. If there was a job or task running, Jenkins will warn you. Select **Yes** because we are not running any jobs yet. Take a look at this screenshot

Are you sure about restarting Jenkins? Jenkins will restart once all running jobs are finished. Yes

Notice that nothing really changed on our host, except that now we have a meme plugin in our plugin index, but no memes. Why is that? Take a look at this screenshot:

Do you remember the principles of plugin usage? The first principle advises us to read and understand the plugin. Back on the documentation, notice that the plugin is only mentioned to work with job builds. Take a look at this screenshot:

Usage

1. Go to the job configuration page and check the "Activate Internet Meme" checkbox in the "Post Build Actions" dropdown
2. Post build run, a random meme image is displayed on the build page.

There are no memes. That's disappointing. We'll get to see our memes when we set up builds.

Activity: Plugin Management

Scenario

You have been asked to prepare your Jenkins server for a simple Continuous Integration build by installing the following plugins:

- Python
- Pyenv
- nodeJS

Aim

To familiarize yourself with resource management.

Steps for Completion

1. Open the **Manage Jenkins** option on the configuration panel. Take a look at this screenshot:

2. Select the **Manage Plugins** option. Take a look at this screenshot:

Manage Plugins
Add, remove, disable or enable plugins that can extend the functionality of Jenkins.

3. Click on the **Available** tab, then on the **Filter** bar, and search for the necessary plugins. Take a look at this screenshot:

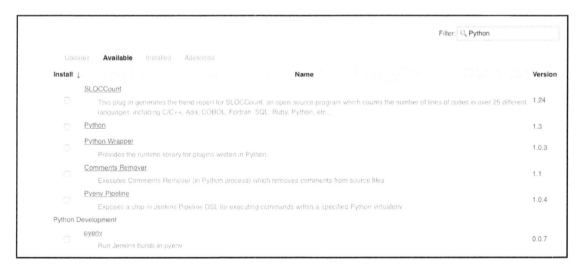

4. Ensure that you confirm the statistical information on the plugin index, which you can also access by clicking on the plugin name. Do this on a new tab.

5. Select the necessary checkboxes, and click on **Install without restart** until you get to the final one, where you will select **Download now and install after restart**. Take a look at this screenshot:

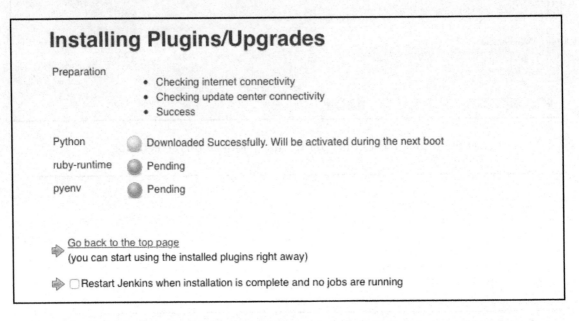

6. Restart Jenkins for the final plugins to take effect. Take a look at this screenshot:

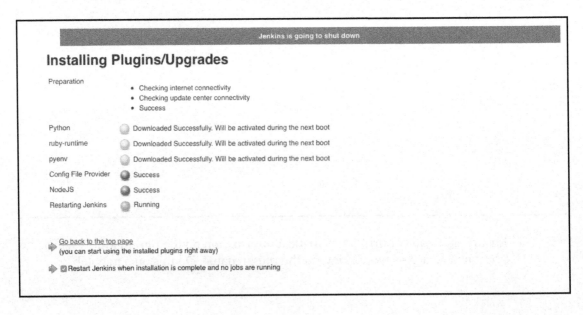

Because we are running locally, this may not work as expected, depending on your internet connection, this is what happened previously. Safe restart your server.

Updating and Upgrading Jenkins

We recently mentioned that Jenkins has a very active community, and because of this, new versions of the server are constantly being released, with a lot of new features and bug fixes. It is highly advisable to always keep the server up to date.

However, the process doesn't really just involve upgrading the host, especially for production servers. There are certain best practices that every administrator, DevOps engineer, and developer needs to follow, to maintain high availability.

In this chapter, we shall walk through the necessary practices and the positive and negative effects of a Jenkins server upgrade. Note that this knowledge is also dynamic to any server upgrade, except of course any Jenkins-related step.

Maintenance Windows

A **maintenance window** is a period of time designated in advance by the technical staff, during which preventive maintenance that could cause disruption of the service may be performed.

 You can read more on maintenance windows at the following link: https://docs.aws.amazon.com/systems-manager/latest/userguide/systems-manager-maintenance.html

To enforce high availability, which aims to avoid downtime, every administrator needs to schedule a window, which ranges from at least biweekly or for, critically engaged services, once every week. This is usually on a weekend. During this period, all stakeholders need to be notified, especially if the service under maintenance is an end-user product.

In any organization, Jenkins will be among the servers at the center of almost all operations. Downtime will have effects not limited to the following:

- Potential feature delivery delays
- Loss of data if any automated builds or processes are operated from Jenkins

- Potential loss of revenue if any scheduled or automated revenue-related service was running
- Potential impact on application services

Now that we recognize the impact of a maintenance window, be sure to at least implement it.

Back to our Jenkins server; what do we need to keep a look out for? This will span quite a number of items, depending on how much Jenkins is used in an organization. In our case, we only need to worry about the following:

- The Jenkins host
- Installed plugins

 If you are running Jenkins as a production host, it is very critical to keep it up to date, but on a stable version. Sometimes, plugins are dependent on a specific version, which raises compatibility issues, eventually leading to unavailability.

If you are going to upgrade the Jenkins host, ensure that you keep a tab on the plugins and, if necessary, upgrade them too. To identify the current Jenkins version, you can check the bottom-right corner on your server page, but this can be found on any page. The version used in this book is 2.89.4, as can be seen from the following screenshot:

REST API   Jenkins ver. 2.89.4

Host Metrics

Host metrics are another good starting point when planning a maintenance period. Why is this? Well, the data collected helps identify problems with the host, and, before the problems become a recurring issue, the administrator can always schedule the host for maintenance. Where do we get these metrics from? We'll look into that in the next section.

Retrieving Jenkins Logs and Metrics

Now we'll analyze how Jenkins handles user management and security.

1. From your dashboard, open **Manage Jenkins** and search for **System Log**. Take a look at this screenshot:

System Log
System log captures output from `java.util.logging` output related to Jenkins.

2. Open the **System Log** file. At this point, we should have at least one log file. Take a look at this screenshot:

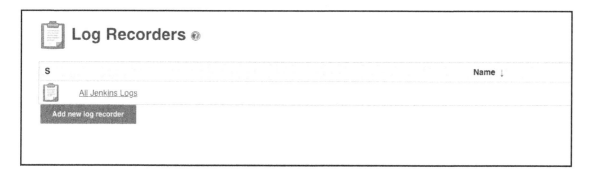

3. Open the log file and observe the output. Take a look at this screenshot:

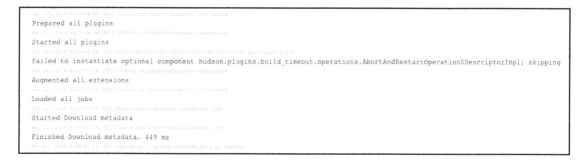

From the output in the file, we can tell that Jenkins keeps a record of all that happens on the host.

If there is ever anything erroring out, Jenkins will capture this and, better yet, there are various ways to capture this and also get notified.

However, it is not recommended to go through logs every single time, especially with multiple nodes running, as this can be very tedious.

Instead, set up a logging framework. This would be the best option in the case of organizations that use Jenkins heavily. Some of these frameworks include, but are not limited to, the following:

- ELK (ElasticSearch, Logstash, and Kibana)
- Graylog

Memory

Memory is a crucial factor that needs to be considered, especially when running any server that collects data. Note that in this case, we are referring to disk space.

Jenkins will collect data from builds, and if the required services are set up, even send out reports in a defined period. This implies that the administrator needs to be aware of the server's memory consumption, which is a very crucial factor to consider during maintenance periods.

Improving Memory Management

We previously talked about log management. Logs are known to be one of the main memory consumers, and if proper care is not enforced, they will take up the memory needed to store logs. A lack of memory to operate causes lag in response and eventually downtime.

To handle this better, on Unix servers, you can enable log rotation. This is a process that manages log files either by compression or deletion in a defined period.

However, even with log rotation, memory is still consumed. An option would be to set up backup databases or datastores, depending on the size of the data that the host consumes. Some of the services available for this are the following:

- Amazon S3
- Cassandra
- Postgres/MongoDB (self-hosted)
- Google's Cloud storage

Upgrading our Jenkins Server

At this point, we are now fairly familiar with the necessary steps and procedures needed to perform a successful upgrade or update. Let's go ahead and check our server.

 Only upgrade your Jenkins server if there is a **stable release** for your current version. **Do not downgrade**. Otherwise, you should feel free to follow through and understand the steps we take from this point forward, until the end of the section.

Head back to the main dashboard, and on the menu, you will see a red just before the search prompt on the right. This is where Jenkins will be sending notifications, so be sure to check any notifications to avoid missing out on critical messages. Take a look at this screenshot:

For now, we shall focus on the upgrade notification, which should be as follows:

It looks as if Jenkins needs an upgrade. Before we even think about upgrading our host, here are a few questions we need to ask:

- Is the recommended version stable?
- Is there any particular reason for upgrading the server?
- Does the recommended version list have any issues that may interfere with current operations and plugins?

Checking the Version Release Notes

Open the **changelog** link in a new tab and notice the release notes at the top, as follows.

Take a look at this screenshot:

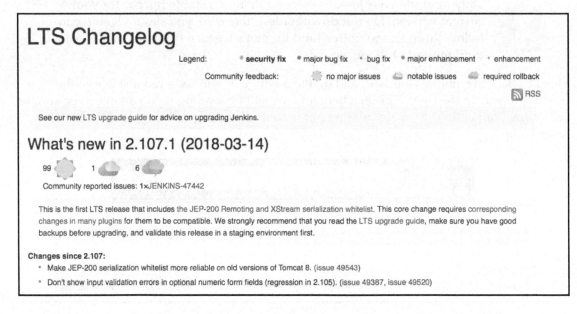

For demonstration purposes, we shall be running this install to get the students familiar with upgrading. Otherwise, we do not have a firm reason to upgrade the server.

Head back to the main dashboard. If you don't have a notification to upgrade, your host should be fine and up to date. Otherwise, we shall be running the automatic upgrade.

1. Ensure that you have no jobs running currently.
2. Select the **Or Upgrade Automatically** button, as follows:

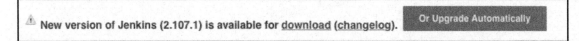

Jenkins will immediately start the download. Take a look at this screenshot:

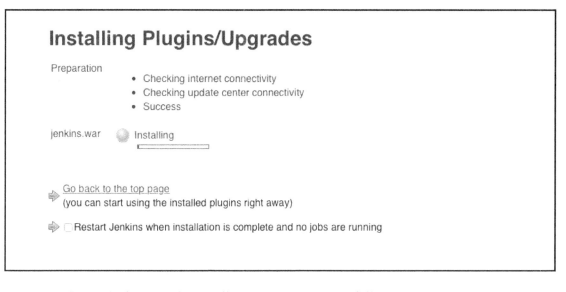

3. Once it's done, Jenkins will prompt a restart, as follows:

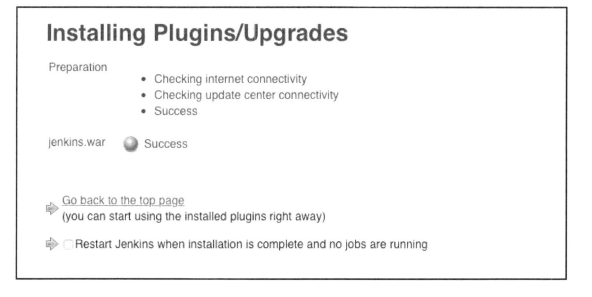

4. Select **Restart Jenkins when installation is complete and no jobs are running**. Take a look at this screenshot:

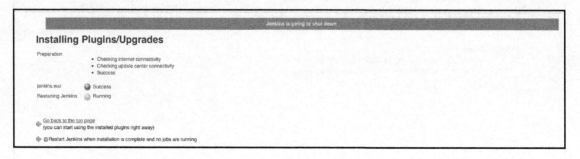

5. Jenkins will restart, and when this is done, you should be prompted to log in or be taken back to the main dashboard.

6. Due to connectivity issues, if the restart loops infinitely, run a safe restart and Jenkins will resume normal operation. Take a look at this screenshot:

7. You should be prompted to go ahead with the restart. Take a look at this screenshot:

Are you sure about restarting Jenkins? Jenkins will restart once all running jobs are finished.

While Jenkins is restarting, notice that in the bottom right corner, our version has moved from 2.89.4 to 2.107.1:

Jenkins ver. 2.107.1

Activity: Upgrades and Updates

Scenario

You have been asked to ensure that your plugins are up to date with stable release versions. Upgrade at least one.

Aim

To familiarize yourself with handling updates and upgrades.

Prerequisites

Ensure that you have the following:

- Jenkins up and running
- You are logged in as the administrator

Steps for Completion

1. Open the **Manage Jenkins** option on the configuration panel. Take a look at this screenshot:

2. Go to the **Manage Plugins** option. Take a look at this screenshot:

Manage Plugins

Add, remove, disable or enable plugins that can extend the functionality of Jenkins.

3. On the **Updates** tab, identify the plugin you want to update. Take a look at this screenshot:

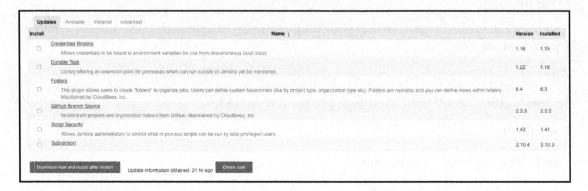

4. Select one from the list. Ensure that you go through the plugin's release notes first, and then click on **Download now and install after restart**. Take a look at this screenshot:

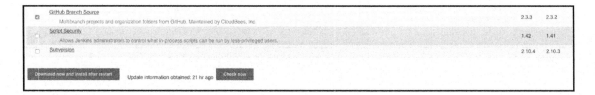

5. Depending on your internet connection, the download will start immediately. Take a look at this screenshot:

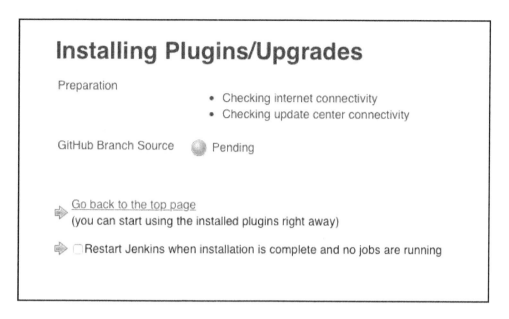

6. Since we are not currently running any jobs, restart Jenkins through the last option for the update to take effect. Take a look at this screenshot:

Configuring Jenkins for Production

Before we define what is needed for a production-like host, let's analyze what we have covered so far:

- We can effectively run and maintain Jenkins.
- We can evaluate what to consider and what to avoid when setting up plugins.
- We can recognize what it takes to have successful server updates and upgrades.
- We can avoid host downtime by following best practices.

Production servers are usually client facing, or in simpler words, web pages that end users actively interact with. Normally, in order to affect a proper production environment, changes need to go through a few more environments for testing and quality assurance. Here are a few examples:

The pages `facebook.com` or `twitter.com` are both production sites. Why is this? Because these are pages that users open to interact with their products.

Their staging environments could be, for example, `staging.facebook.com` or `staging.twitter.com`. End users won't have access to these, because this is where final changes are tested before they appear on the production sites, for example, new user interface features.

In our case, we wouldn't need a staging, QA, or test Jenkins environment. This is also because Jenkins ensures that the right features and integrations get to production and other environments, and thus this is a production environment itself and the center of all other operations.

A few best practices mentioned on the Jenkins wiki for production environments include the following:

- Security
- Access limited to the master node (we shall delve deeper into this later in the book)
- Backup of Jenkins Home
- Project naming conventions should be followed
- Getting rid of jobs and resources that are not in use

Evaluating our Jenkins Server

Since our server is currently for demonstration purposes, we will not be able to fully achieve a production environment. However, we will explore all of the requirements. Without proper care, some of the implications would include the following:

- Vulnerability to hackers
- Data loss
- Attacks such as **man-in-the-middle attacks**, where traffic is stolen through the imitation and replication of servers

Now we'll test the security of our Jenkins server.

1. Go to **Manage Jenkins**. Take a look at this screenshot:

2. Select **Configure System**. Take a look at this screenshot:

3. Under **Jenkins Location**, we have our server address. Take a look at this screenshot:

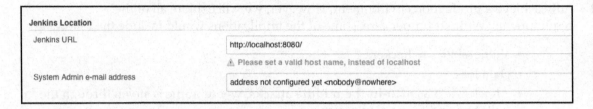

Jenkins Location	
Jenkins URL	http://localhost:8080/
	⚠ Please set a valid host name, instead of localhost
System Admin e-mail address	address not configured yet <nobody@nowhere>

 To enforce security, we would need to host Jenkins and a few recommended services including but not limited to the following: Amazon EC2, Google's Compute Engine, and Digital Ocean Droplets.

We would also need to get **SSL certificates** and a domain name. Above all that, we can also enforce our server in a VPC, where only people with access to the network can actually get to the Jenkins server. **SSL Certificates** activate a secure protocol to the server and allow secure connections.

Access Points

Access points are methods, channels, or ways users can open or access a specific service. These points are vital to what service is offered and can have implications if not properly managed.

Currently, Jenkins can be accessed either through the UI or through Docker, by SSH. In a production environment, connections would be strictly limited to a specific port number and user interface.

Let's have a look at which ports are open. Head on to **Configure Global Security**, under **Manage Jenkins**.

Under **SSH Server**, notice that this feature has been disabled. Take a look at this screenshot:

In a production environment, we would have a default of 22 or any of your choice, depending on usage. Always be sure to limit the number of ports open.

Access Control

Access Control involves limiting privileges to a service and a number of people. This means having measures set in place that restrict only certain people to a resource on a server, or the server itself.

There is something wrong here. Can you identify the problem?

Here's a clue. **Remember me on this computer** is the issue we need to get rid of. Why is this?

If at any time an unauthorized person gets access to your computer, they would have access to Jenkins and everything running on the server. This includes all keys, certificates, and data. This should never happen, and on that note, let's fix this issue.

Testing the Access Control

Now we'll test the access control of Jenkins server.

1. Go to **Manage Jenkins**. Take a look at this screenshot:

2. Under **Configure Global Security**, select the checkbox next to **Disable remember me**. Take a look at this screenshot:

3. Click **Apply** then **Save**. Log out, and your display should be as follows:

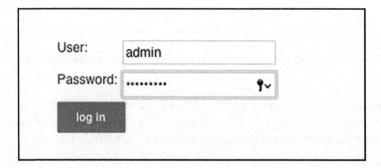

This implies that only authorized and authenticated users can access Jenkins, and that operations are strictly limited to access levels. This means that certain users are limited to specific operations.

Services and Plugins

Although not as crucial as access control, every administrator needs to be aware of the services and plugins integrated into Jenkins, what they do, and what they have access to.

A year ago, JavaScript developers were shocked to find out a few node packages were collecting useful data like credit cards from unaware developers, which really shook the trust in open source code. This is why everyone needs to pay attention to the information on a package's documentation, in order to avoid such occurrences.

 Always seek to understand what a plugin does before installing it, because setting it up could be as good as giving up all your data.

Summary

In this chapter, we covered setting up and managing plugins the right way. We updated and upgraded Jenkins the proper way, considering its urgency and implications.

Then, we enforced security in our Jenkins server by identifying common vulnerability points. Then, we followed the recommended practices when managing data on Jenkins, identifying the best practices and tools. Finally, we ran demos on practices for setting up production servers.

Now that we understand how to manage our server and its resources, we can confidently prepare our host for any operation or service, whether it's a new language we want to set up projects for, or a service that directly interacts with an already existing project. The next chapter will help us fully prepare and understand the entire process by introducing freestyle projects and Jenkins views for freestyle projects.

3
Jenkins Views and Freestyle Projects

In the previous chapters, we explored Jenkins inside out. To be more precise, we have been able to achieve the following:

- Set up Jenkins on Docker
- Add users and limit their access
- Set up build and user interface-related plugins
- Demonstrate how to update and upgrade Jenkins
- Recognize what is needed to achieve a production-like Jenkins server

We can now comfortably manage Jenkins and its resources in the proper way. This chapter will focus on the build we described earlier in Chapter 2, *Administering Jenkins*. We shall demonstrate and implement build management through Python examples.

Do not be alarmed if you have no previous experience with the language, as we shall only cover need-to-know information related to Jenkins.

The process of build management enables a number of crucial operations, such as bug and error detection, and also serves as one of the most critical automatable processes. As an administrator or DevOps engineer, you need to be at least conversant with what is synonymous in different language builds. The most trending languages in the market are as follows:

- Go
- Java
- JavaScript (Node.js and frameworks including React, Angular, and Vue.js)
- Python
- Ruby

These are the most common languages most developers deal with. You may recall setting up a few plugins related to Python in the previous chapter. Python is one of the easiest languages to set up.

By the end of this chapter, you will be able to:

- Recognize how Jenkins works with version control
- Implement freestyle projects
- Identify how Jenkins' separation of concern improves product health
- Implement views for Jenkins projects

Freestyle Projects

Freestyle means improvised or unrestricted. A freestyle project in Jenkins is a project that spans multiple operations. It can be a build, a script run, or even a pipeline.

According to the official Jenkins wiki, a freestyle project is a typical build job or task. This could be as simple as running tests, building or packaging an application, sending a report, or even running some commands. Before any tests are run, data is collated. This can also be done by Jenkins. Jenkins collects data through multiple ways depending on what is being achieved and the purpose of the data in question. A real-world scenario could involve, for instance, the collection of application artifacts after builds. In relation to management, Jenkins allows us to send reports at any defined stage, which could entail artifact information, or shipping application logs to a log management entity, such as Elasticsearch.

In the previous chapter, we highlighted what a Continuous Integration pipeline would entail, and how Jenkins handles code through the pipeline. This chapter will now demonstrate this through builds, eventually building on pipelines as we progress.

As a prerequisite, we assume that everyone will have the required knowledge needed to set up freestyle projects of different kinds, including:

- **Application Builds**: These enable applications to be bundled and packaged
- **Test jobs**: These enable application tests to be run
- **Script runs**: These enable various processes to be run such as report delivery and command executions

Setting up Freestyle Projects

Let's try and set up freestyle projects using Jenkins. You need to first ensure that you have Jenkins up and running, and that you are authenticated as the admin. To set up a freestyle project, follow these steps:

1. Open the main dashboard to create a project using the **New Item** option on the left navigation menu.

If still available, you may also use the **create new jobs** prompt to create a project, as seen here:

Welcome to Jenkins!

Please **create new jobs** to get started.

Here's what the menu looks like:

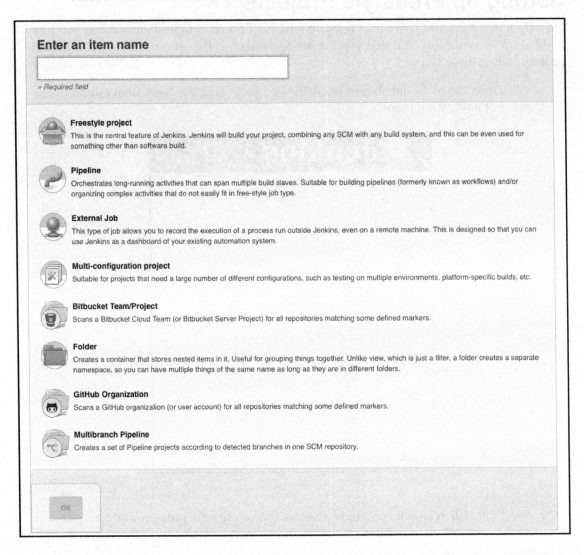

The view above presents the various job types Jenkins supports. This chapter shall solely focus on **Freestyle projects**, but we will however look into more jobs and items as we progress.

2. Enter the name as `jenkins-python-run` and select **Freestyle project** as highlighted in the following screenshot, and then select **OK**.

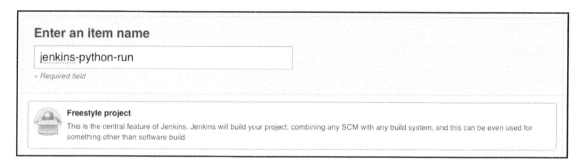

Jenkins should automatically take you to the project configuration view. All content can be quickly accessed through the tabs. Take a look at this screenshot:

We'll have a look at all the content step by step. For now, let's understand what the **Source Code Management** resource does. This checks out code from version control hosts. This means that if your code is hosted on GitHub or any other web-based repositories, you can add the repository details and Jenkins will clone it.

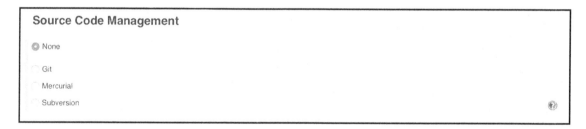

Feel free to use the quick tips displayed in the blue question mark icons, as they can be very resourceful and provide more clarification.

3. Select **Git** and the following menu should drop down. This entails the information needed to clone a Git repository.

4. Let's get the repository we are going to build from GitHub. From your browser, head to the following address `https://github.com/TrainingByPackt/` `Beginning-Jenkins`.

   From the repository, notice that we are on the master branch. Take a look at this screenshot:

5. Select the **Clone or download** button and copy the link, as shown in the following screenshot:

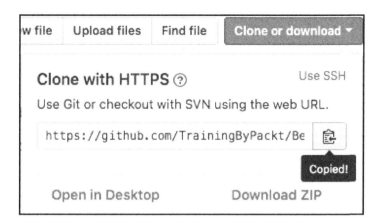

This is the link Jenkins will use to clone the repository in order to run our tests.

6. Back on our project configuration, add the repository link as follows:

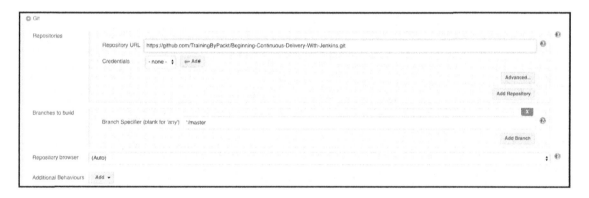

 For now, this is all we need to do to clone a public repository from GitHub. Private repositories need extra authentication, so be sure to provide credentials on the **Credentials** field. We will cover this in a later chapter.

Now, let's get back to examining what the rest of the tabs in the project configuration view do. The **Build Triggers** resource helps in automating builds. When setting up pipelines, some of the processes need to be automated in order to be effective. Some of these processes may include build and deploy steps:

Build Triggers

Build Triggers

☐ Trigger builds remotely (e.g., from scripts)

☐ Build after other projects are built

☐ Build periodically

☐ GitHub hook trigger for GITScm polling

☐ Poll SCM

When changes are pushed to GitHub, Jenkins should automatically run tests and build applications instead of developers triggering manual builds each time. More of this will be covered in the next section.

The **Build Environment** resource, as its name suggests, is involved with the environment–more precisely, the application environment. Credentials need to be set to, for example, access a server; a language-specific detail, such as Python virtual environments; and project management resources such as ticket tags:

Build Environment

☐ Delete workspace before build starts

☐ Use secret text(s) or file(s)

☐ Abort the build if it's stuck

☐ Add timestamps to the Console Output

☐ Generate Release Notes

☐ With Ant

☐ pyenv build wrapper

Under the **Build** menu, you will find the drop-down with the following options:

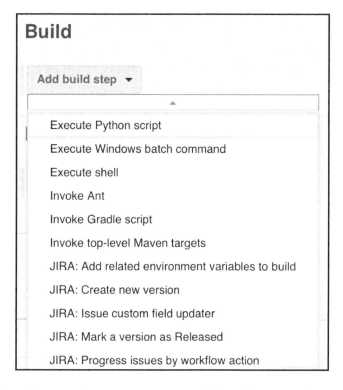

This resource defines the actual steps we want to achieve, for example:

- Do you want to run a script?
- Do you want to run a command?

 This step can be extended by installing plugins, and some of those steps might vary depending on the Jenkins version running and/or the installed plugins.

The **Post-Build Actions** are actions you want to do after a task is done. For instance, if you were running tests on the Build option, you could:

- Send an email notification
- Generate and send a report

Setting up the Build

Now that we've set up a freestyle project, let's set up our build environment. Follow these steps:

1. On the project configuration page, select **Apply** and then **Save**. This should take you to the following page.

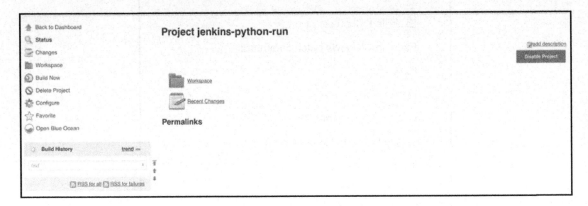

2. Select **Build Now** on the left navigation menu to run the build.

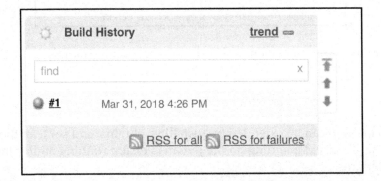

Notice that a number pops up on the **Build History**. Hover over the build number and select the drop-down list. This presents a quick menu for your builds. Open the **Console Output** to view the logs of our build, as shown here:

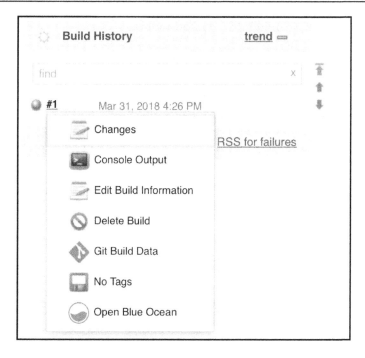

3. Hover over the number to get a drop-down, and select **Console Output** to view the build logs. The logs will tell us what happened when our code was being pulled, and if the build has an issue, this is the quickest way to identify it. Your window should have an output that's similar to the following:

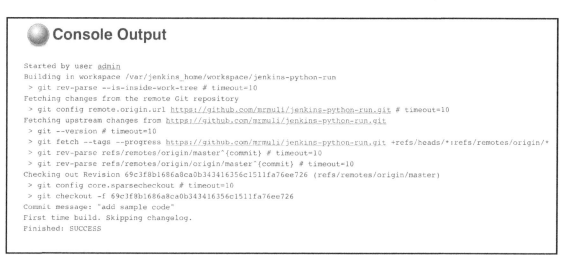

From the logs, we can identify the following:

- Who triggered the build
- The commands that were run to achieve the build's purpose
- Any changes made
- Whether the build was a **Success** or a **Fail**

We haven't run any code or tests, so let's go ahead and complete our build by adding this.

4. Select **Back to Project** and then **Configure**, on the left navigation menu, which should take us back to the project configuration page.

    In our case, we want Jenkins to run our tests from the tests.py file. In an ideal local environment, we would run the tests on the terminal or by using Git Bash:

```
→ jenkins-python-run git:(master) python tests.py
..
-------------------------------------------------------------------------
Ran 2 tests in 0.000s

OK
```

5. Under **Build**, select **Add build step**. This will enable us to add a step for Jenkins to run our tests.

We will choose **Shell**, even though we are running Jenkins on Windows. Why? Because Jenkins is running on a Docker container, which has a Linux operating system by default.

To achieve the same result, we will need to tell Jenkins to run the script, as we saw on the preceding terminal. This can be achieved by selecting **Execute shell** from the **Add build step** drop-down. With this in mind, we can execute any kind of script, provided the necessary languages or tools are available on the Docker container. We are executing a shell, even though we are on a Windows operating system, because Jenkins is running in a Docker container:

6. Select **Execute shell** and the following window should pop up.

You can add as many build steps as required. For post-build items, it's preferred to use the **Post-build Actions** resource.

Since this is the first time we are running Python scripts on Jenkins, despite having the Python plugin, we also need to install Python. Why? Because the Docker Container doesn't come with Python pre-installed.

7. Add the commands on the prompt, as follows:

8. Select **Apply**, then **Save**. This will take you back to the project window.
9. On the left navigation menu, select **Build Now** to build the project.

   Jenkins will automatically schedule the build and display a new build number on the **Build History** pane, as shown:

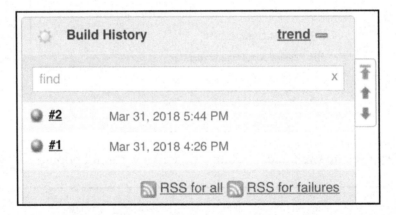

Now, go ahead and open the **Console Output** and view the logs. Since Python is already set up on this container, the output shown here won't display the logs; however, the test results will be displayed as follows:

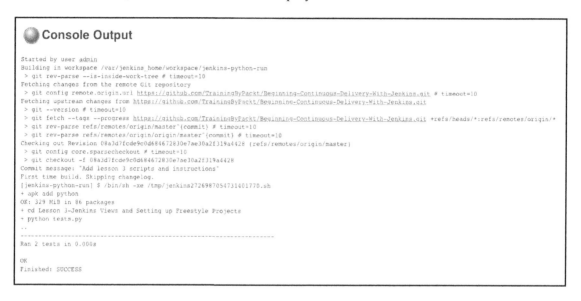

Congratulations! We now have a complete build. Let's quickly recap what our build entails:

1. Jenkins will first pull the code from GitHub after we add the repository details.
2. Through the build step, Jenkins will run the Python script.
3. The logs on the console output tell us whether our build has failed or passed.

As we progress, we will get to understand how to set up more complex builds that can be triggered automatically and even send notifications.

Back on the main dashboard, notice how Jenkins has updated to factor in our build. We can now easily view and access our build(s), and on the left navigation menu, we can also view any build that is queued.

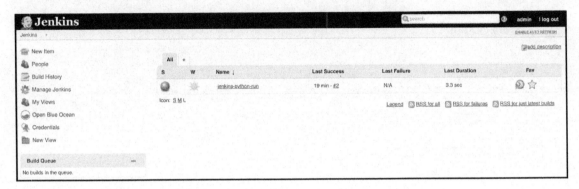

We will discuss views in the next section.

Activity: Setting up a Freestyle Project

Scenario

You have been asked to set up a freestyle project so that you can run a script via Jenkins from the repository link given below:

1. The script name is `sample.py` and the response should be **Hello World**.
2. Access the repository from the following link `https://github.com/TrainingByPackt/Beginning-Jenkins/tree/master/Lesson3`.

Aim

To set up the freestyle project dashboard to access developer views and job

Prerequisites

Ensure that everyone has Jenkins up and running, and is authenticated as the admin.

Steps for Completion

1. Log in as the **Administrator**.
2. On the Dashboard, select the **New Item** option on the configuration panel.

3. Name the project as shown in the screenshot.

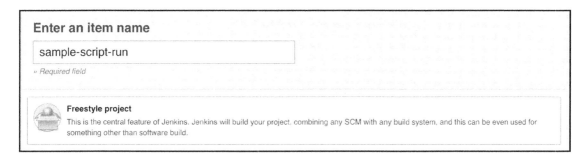

4. Under **Source Code Management**, select **Git** and add the repository URL as shown:

5. Under **Build**, add the command to run the script. This time around, we won't be installing Python as it should be up and running from the previous install.

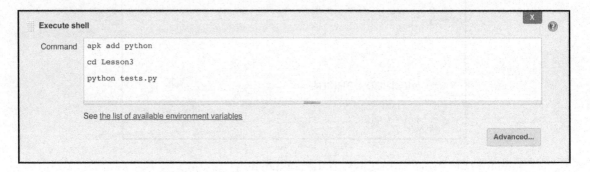

6. Click **Apply** and **Save**.
7. On the left navigation menu, select the **Build Now** option and the script should run.

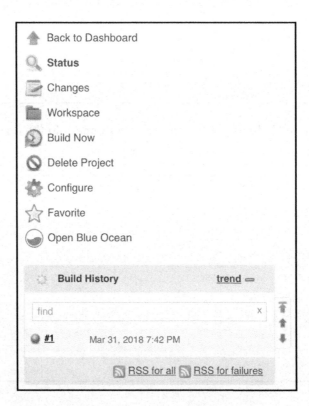

8. Open the build console and observe the logs. The message **Hello World!** should be outputted on the console.

Setting up a View to Manage our Projects

A Jenkins view is basically the display or table that lists our projects. The option lists our projects on the dashboard, as shown:

Views allow us to organize and manage projects better. They help in classifying projects according to the merit that's defined, for example, purpose. Generally, views allow us to organize and manage projects better, whether they are freestyle projects or pipeline jobs. When we start adding more projects to our Jenkins server, the default dashboard view won't be as sustainable. Imagine the effort you would spend scrolling over 100 projects?

Jenkins folders can also be used alongside views to make navigation easier.

In this section, we will demonstrate how we can improve this experience and categorize our jobs in different views.

View Permissions

Throughout this book, we have been the **Administrator**. Everything we set up or want to set up will probably work. Why? Because the administrator has all the permissions. We were also able to create some users and set up permissions according to their roles. This time around, we are going to give the developer (dev1) more permissions to views and various jobs. We are doing this so that the developer doesn't have to contact the administrator or open a helpdesk ticket every time he/she wants to debug a failed build or just check on its progress.

Here's the developer's current view. They can only view as far as the dashboard and the users present in the server:

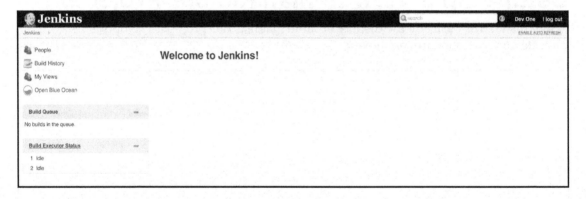

If your permissions are as we configured them in Chapter 1, *Installing and Setting up Jenkins*, the developer should get an error when creating a job or accessing anything beyond the **Overall Read Permission**:

Log back in as the **Administrator** and head on to **Configure Global Security** under **Manage Jenkins**. We are going to allow the developer to do the following:

- Read views
- Read jobs

We want the developer to only access different jobs (builds) grouped into different views. Keep this in mind, as we'll cover this in more detail in the next section. The Administrator and DevOps engineers still remain the only users who can create views according to project specs.

 It's important to enforce this separation of concern among teams because everyone gets to focus and perfect on their field and are united under the same goal and objectives. This increases product delivery pace and enhances quality. Separation of concern gives everyone a sense of ownership and focus towards specific tasks, meaning everyone gets to focus on their responsibilities, enabling a healthier product.

Setting up Jenkins Views Privileges

To set up the privilege views in Jenkins, follow these steps:

1. Under **Manage Jenkins**, select **Configure Global Security**.
2. Under the Authorization type **Matrix based Security**, update the developer's permissions to include reading views and jobs, as depicted in the following screenshot:

	Job									Run			View			
	Build	Cancel	Configure	Create	Delete	Discover	Move	Read	Workspace	Delete	Replay	Update	Configure	Create	Delete	Read
	✓	✓	✓	✓	✓	✓	✓	✓	✓	✓	✓	✓	✓	✓	✓	✓
								✓								✓
	✓	✓	✓	✓	✓	✓	✓	✓	✓	✓	✓	✓	✓	✓	✓	✓

 The middle row is the developer, with only Job read, View read, and the Overall Read permissions, which we set up earlier. This one won't change. To understand the permissions better, read through the following link: https://jenkins.io/doc/book/managing/security/.

3. Click **Apply**, then **Save**.
4. On logging back in as the developer, we will now be able to access jobs and views. Note that we can only **Read** them.

Setting up Views

From the Dashboard, views can be added in two ways. Before we proceed, can you notice any differences in the developer view compared to the administrator view?

As the administrator, notice the view bar just above the first job:

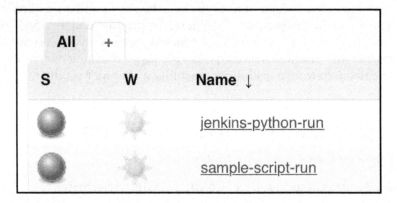

Here's the developer's view:

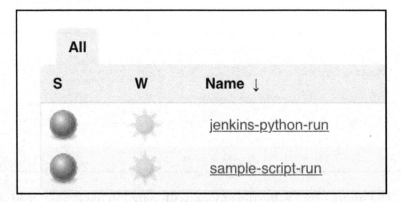

Do you see any difference? The "+" sign allows us to create views.

Now, let's understand how to set up views in Jenkins. We need to perform the following steps:

1. Use the left navigation menu to add more views by selecting **New View**. Go ahead and select this option:

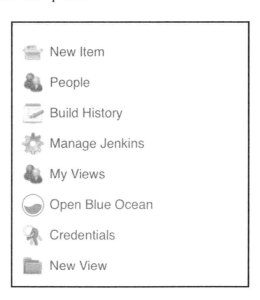

We should be navigated to the view configuration page, where there's the following:

- **List View**: This view simply shows jobs or items in a list, and you can group jobs according to projects, vendors, or any category you prefer.
- **My View**: This view automatically displays all jobs you have access to:

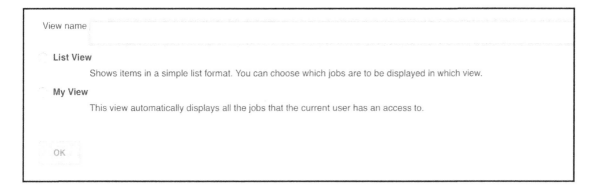

These are the default view types Jenkins is bundled with. You can always set up plugins that support more views in your preferences.

2. Add the name `testing`, select **List View**, and proceed with **OK**. This should navigate you to the view configuration page.

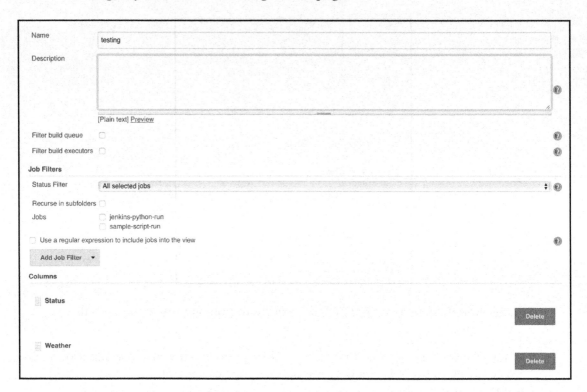

As per the various configuration options, here is what we want to achieve: A view that displays only jobs that run tests. You can also set up a view for specific environment jobs, for example, staging or production.

3. Update the description as follows:

By checking **Filter build queue** and/or **Filter build executors**, we only want to see resources related to this specific view, for example, only this view's jobs on the queue:

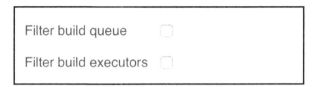

4. Under **Job Filters**, select the `jenkins-python-run` job, which is the one we ran tests on.

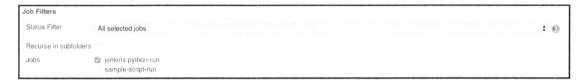

5. Finally, under **Columns**, add or remove the columns according to your preference. For demonstration purposes, we will be maintaining all columns.
6. Click **Apply**, then select **OK**.

This will automatically redirect you to the main dashboard view and, alas, we have a testing-specific view.

The developer is also able to access this view. On that note, developers have easier access to specific items. This means that if anyone has the need to check on test builds, they can directly access the `testing` view and identify the job.

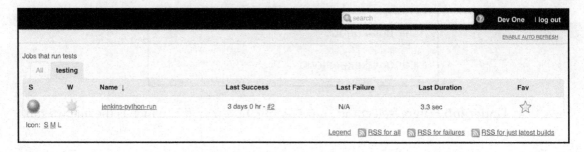

Activity: Setting up a View to Manage our Projects

Scenario

You have been asked to set up a `miscellaneous` view, which includes jobs that do everything but run tests.

Aim

To set up a freestyle project dashboard to categorize developer jobs and views

Prerequisites

Ensure that you have the following:

1. Jenkins up and running.
2. You are logged in as the **Administrator**.
3. You have a developer user profile with the following permissions:
    - Is able to access views
    - Is able to access jobs
    - Has the overall read permission

Steps for Completion

1. On the left navigation menu, select **New View**.

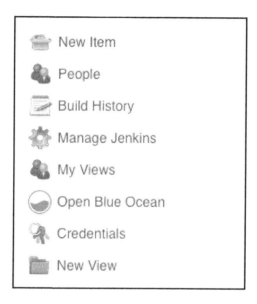

2. Select **List View** and put the **View** name as `miscellaneous`.

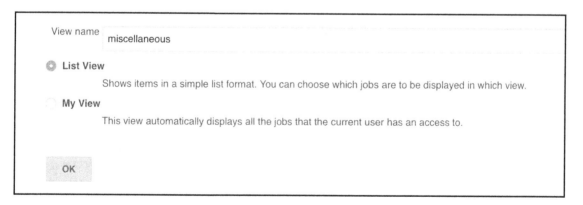

3. Update the view's description and select the job(s), as shown in the below screenshot:

4. Update the **Columns** where necessary, and then click **Apply** and **Save**.
5. The view should be listed on the dashboard, and with it, the job(s).

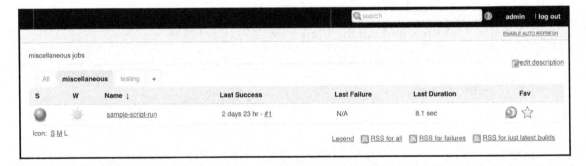

6. Verify that the developer is able to access the views and jobs.

Summary

In this chapter, we defined and implemented examples of freestyle projects that run scripts. We then demonstrated how to set up script builds on Jenkins. Lastly, we identified what it takes to make build environments more convenient and efficient through views.

We can now confidently set up freestyle projects to run tasks as simple as test runs and/or application builds. In the following chapter, we will delve deeper into automating freestyle projects. This will involve setting up parameterized builds and configuring upstream and downstream projects.

4
Parameterized and Up/Downstream Project

In the previous chapters, we managed to cover the following:

- Installing and setting up Jenkins on different environments
- How to administer and secure Jenkins once installed on our environment
- Creating freestyle projects and customizing the Jenkins interface with views

While working on a project locally, for instance, a project that needs access to a development database or, say, some credentials to access a specific service, we provide access to this by setting environment variables on our development machines. When running this same project on Jenkins for testing, we need a mechanism to provide access to these same services to the project as it runs on our build server. Builds or build jobs are the core of the Jenkins build process. Jenkins creates a build for every change made in the code repository. Build jobs are used to process other tasks, such as deploying an application to a server. To achieve this, we use build parameters.

Build parameters help us set environment variables for our projects, which they can in turn access as the build runs. For instance, you could have a test database hosted on a database as a service platform that your tests run against; you would use a build parameter to provide access to this.

In this chapter, we shall begin to explore some of the features offered by Jenkins when running our projects, to make them more customizable to fit different scenarios and to make our builds run in different ways based on the values assigned to the parameters.

By the end of this chapter, you will be able to:

- Explain what build parameters are and their importance
- Modify parameters of our freestyle projects
- Create upstream and downstream projects

Configuring Parameters for Projects

It is essential to configure the parameters of our project so that it is optimized to the task to be performed. A build parameter is a predefined value or a value configured before running a build. This is important as it enables you to customize your builds to make them fit different scenarios and also secure your secrets compared to storing them on version control. Build jobs are used to process related tasks, such as deploying applications to a server or running integration tests. This is a benefit to private companies such as Dell, NASA, and so on, and to open source projects such as Mozilla and AngularJS.

In both of the preceding scenarios, we can make use of build parameters to customize our build to make it run differently depending on what we pass in as the parameter prior to running the build.

Parameterized Projects

Let's now create our first parameterized project using Jenkins. Follow the steps given below:

1. On the Jenkins dashboard, select **New Item** on the top left of the dashboard (the first item on the side menu).

2. On the next page, select **Freestyle project** as the project type. Insert an appropriate name for the project, as depicted in the following screenshot, and then press the **OK** button right below the project types.

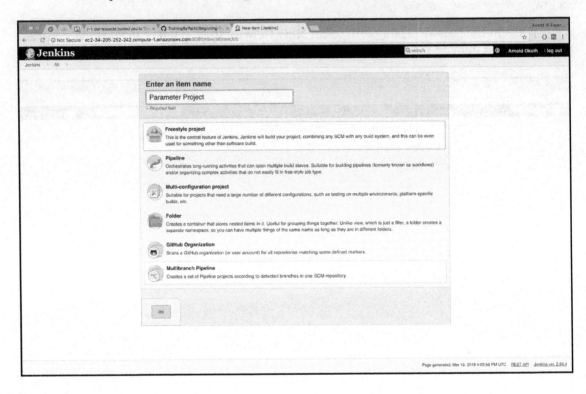

3. After the successful creation of the project, you will land on the following page:

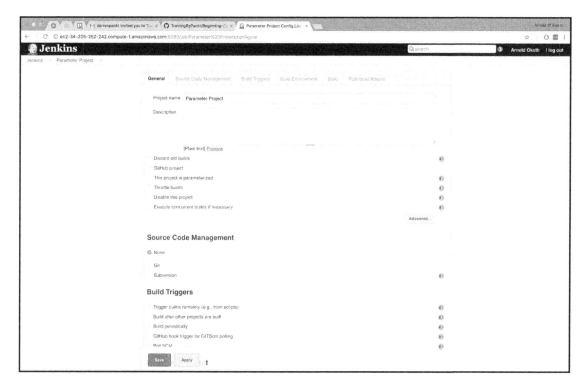

You can choose to add a description in the description text field describing what the project does.

At this point, we have to tell Jenkins that we want to add parameters to our project. Below the description text field, there is a list of checkboxes. The third one on the list reads **This project is parameterized**; enable this option and your view will change, as shown in the following screenshot:

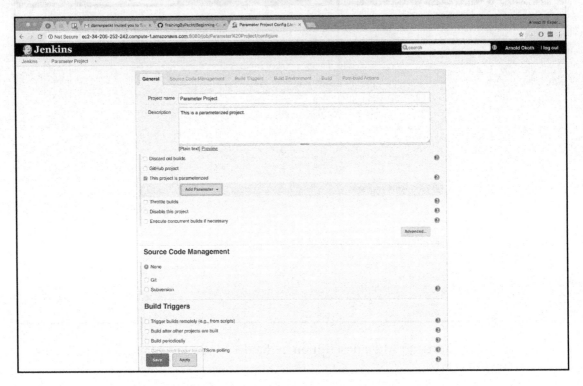

Jenkins is well documented, with really helpful prompts in appropriate places. At this point, we are interested in the third item on the list, but if you want to find out what the rest of the items are, you can click the question mark icon on the right and Jenkins will give you a hint as to what the effect of enabling those checkboxes would be.

4. The **Add Parameter** button appears right below the previously enabled checkbox. Once we click on it, Jenkins shows us the different types of parameters we can use in our projects, as follows:

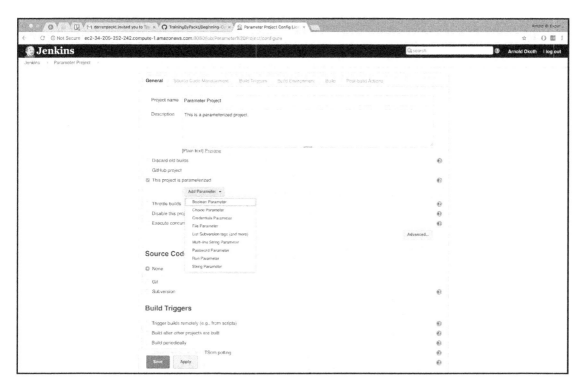

The following are the different types of build parameters that Jenkins supports:

Boolean: A Boolean parameter can contain either true or false. A good use case for this is controlling the flow of your build scripts; for example, depending on the value of a given Boolean parameter, the build script can take a given action.

Choice: A choice parameter takes in a list of different options that you can select from prior to running the build. This can be used to configure different flags for a build script and you can select which options you want as you run the build.

Credentials: One of the most commonly used build parameters is the credentials parameter. This is used to configure sensitive credentials such as SSH private keys, a username/password, and so on.

File: A file parameter is also very common and allows you to pass in a file or artifact to a build and configure the build to run some actions against it. This enables you to produce artifacts locally and upload them to Jenkins for different purposes, which can greatly reduce the build time on your Jenkins server.

List subversion tags: This parameter is used together with version control to allow the user to create a project from a tag from which Jenkins will create a working copy and perform the configured build tasks.

String: This defines a simple text parameter, where users can enter a string value, which you can use during a build, either as an environment variable, or through variable substitution in some other parts of the configuration.

Multiline string: A multiline string is a string that spans multiple lines and a good use case would be release notes to go along with your build artifact when running a deployment.

Password: A password is a simple text parameter that differentiates itself from the string parameter by the fact that the input value is obfuscated.

Run: A run parameter allows users to pick a single run of a specific project. This can be used during the build to query Jenkins for further information.

Thus, by using such build parameters, we can store configuration options or data that is not a part of the source code.

Creating and Accessing Build Parameters

In the previous section, we covered how to create parameterized projects and the different types of build parameters that are supported on Jenkins. In this section, we will create some of the build parameters and learn how to access them. As mentioned earlier, build parameters enable us to accomplish various things, such as providing our build with a database connection string to grant it credentials to access various services, for example, a deployment token, and so on.

Creating and Accessing String Parameters

Let's now understand how to create and access string parameters with Jenkins. Follow the steps given below:

1. On the dashboard, click on the **Parameter Project** we created in the previous section and navigate to the configuration page by clicking on the **Configure** hyperlink on the menu on the left.

2. Ensure that the **This project is parameterized** checkbox is enabled. We can now go ahead and create string parameters.

3. Click on **Add Parameter** and select **String Parameter**.

   A form will appear, as shown in the following screenshot, asking you for the name, default value, and a description of the parameter:

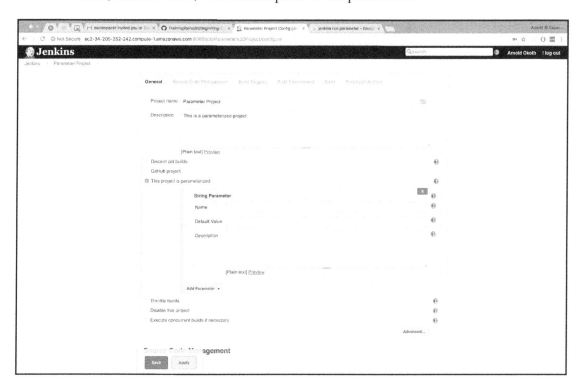

4. Fill the form, as shown in the following screenshot, supplying the **Name** as PARAM1, **Default Value** as Parameter One, and a random description:

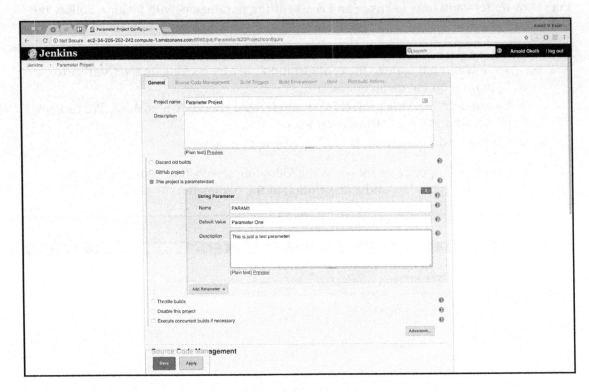

5. Click **Apply** at the bottom of the screen to save the changes and a green prompt will appear at the top of your dashboard displaying the message that you have successfully saved the changes you made.

6. While on the same page, click on **Build** on the main menu of the project configuration. The view will scroll down and look like the following:

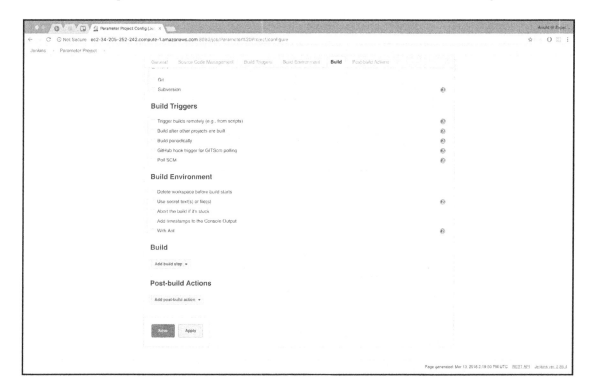

After creating build parameters on Jenkins, we can access them like normal environment variables using a shell script. A shell script is a program designed to be run using the interactive Unix command-line interpreter and is written using bash syntax. Read more about shell scripting at `https://www.tldp.org/guides.html`.

We will be using a shell script as a build step to display or access our build parameters.

7. Under the **Build** title, select the **Add Build Step** drop-down menu and select **Execute Shell**, as shown in the following screenshot:

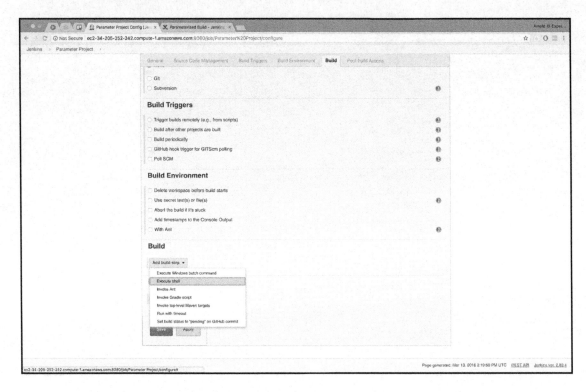

You will be presented with a text area for adding the shell command that you want to execute. We'll insert a very simple command that will just display the build parameter we created earlier.

8. Enter the command `echo $PARAM1` in the text area, as shown in the below screenshot. This will output the value `PARAM1` during the build.

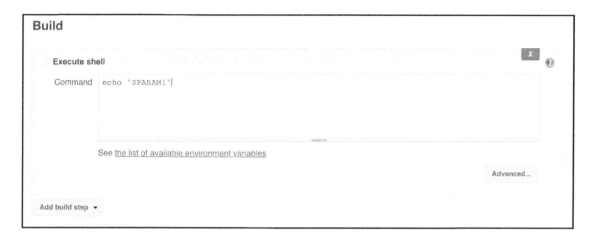

9. Click **Apply** and **Save** at the bottom of the screen and Jenkins will take you back to the project's dashboard, as shown in the following screenshot:

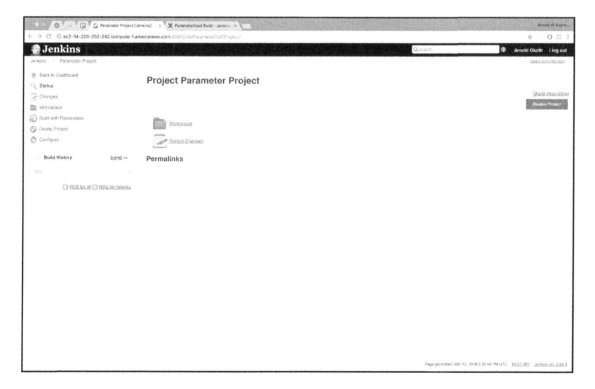

At this point, we want to build our project and run the configuration we just created. Since our project is parameterized, there is a **Build with Parameters** option on the left-hand menu, which is the fifth item.

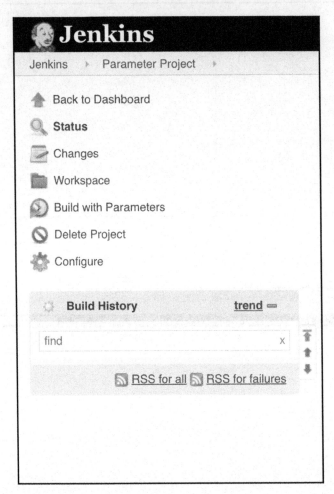

The following page will be presented after you select that option:

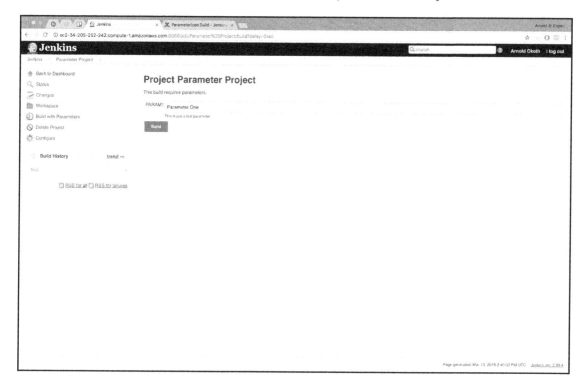

As shown in the above screenshot, we are prompted to supply a value for the parameter we created and the text field is already filled with the default value we have defined. We can opt to supply a different value or just build the project with the default value, which is exactly what we will do.

10. Click on the **Build** button and, after doing so, we see the page shown in the following screenshot:

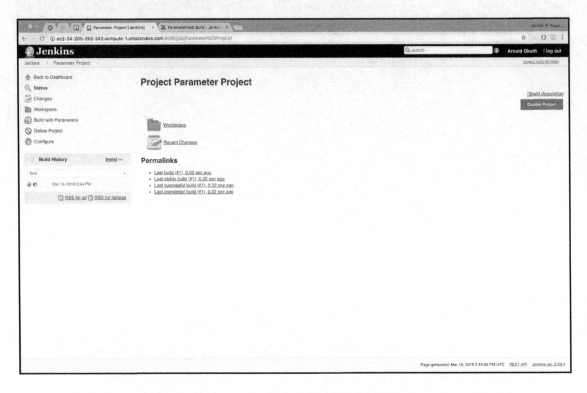

Due to the simplicity of our project, our build should take a short time to run. Since this was our first build, on the left-hand side of the screen, right under our menu, we can see the **Build History** and **#1** on the side. This confirms that this is our first build, that is, build **#1,** and a timestamp of when our build ran.

11. To view the output of our build, we can hover the mouse pointer over build number **#1** and a down-facing arrow will appear. Click on the arrow and select the **Console Output** option, as shown in the following screenshot:

12. After selecting the **Console Output** option, we are presented with the following:

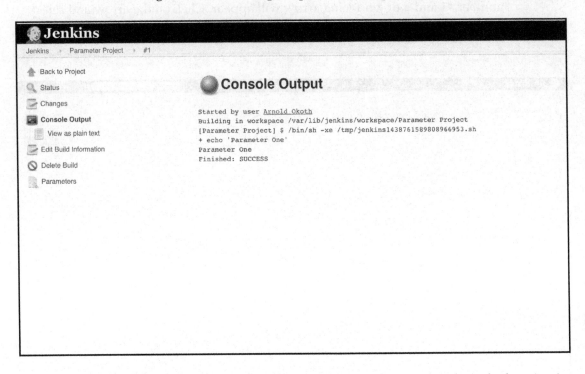

The output displays the user who started the build on the first line, the location in which the build is running, and the script that ran, which we created earlier, in our build step.

Our Bash script is running in debug mode as defined in the `/bin/sh -xe`. Read more about Bash flags at `https://www.tldp.org/LDP/abs/html/options.html`.

The last three lines display the command that was run, the output of the command, and the status of the build, that is, whether it was successful or not. As we can see, the output was `Parameter One`. The build will display what we configured as the value of our build parameter, that is, `PARAM1`.

In this section, we have gone through how to create parameterized projects in Jenkins and also how to access them through shell commands. We have also learned that build parameters are essential when running real-world projects to make them more flexible and customizable; they are also essential for security, since they allow you to store sensitive data on your Jenkins server. We will get to see how build parameters come together in a real project with an activity in later chapters.

Activity: Setting up Parameterized Projects and Accessing Parameters

Scenario

You have been asked to set up a freestyle project that will contain two string parameters, your first and last names, and a build step executing a bash script that will display the greeting **Hello** followed by your full name.

Aim

To set up parameterized projects and access parameters

Prerequisites

Ensure the following:

- Jenkins is up and running
- You are logged in as the **Administrator**

Steps for Completion

1. On the Jenkins dashboard, go to the configuration panel and select **New Item**.

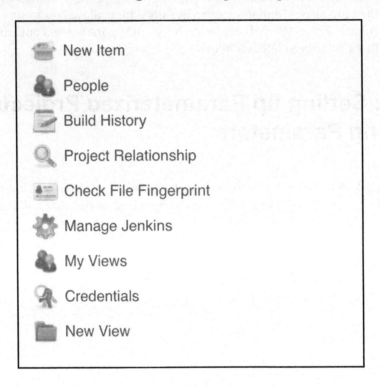

2. On the **New Item** view, enter a project name, select **Freestyle project**, then select **OK**.

3. Under the general section of the project configuration, enter an appropriate project description.

4. Enable the checkbox **This project is parameterized** to allow you to add parameters to the project, as shown in the following screenshot:

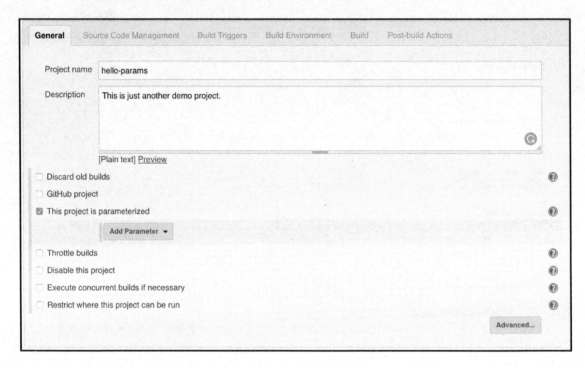

5. Add the first parameter by clicking on the **Add Parameter** drop-down menu and selecting **String Parameter**, as shown in the following screenshot:

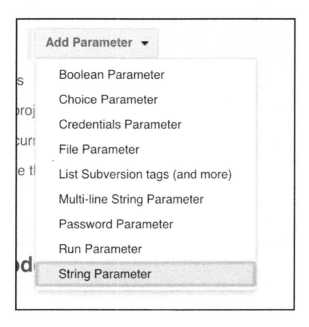

6. Fill in the form with the details of the first parameter, that is, your first name, as displayed. This will present us with the form shown in the following screenshot:

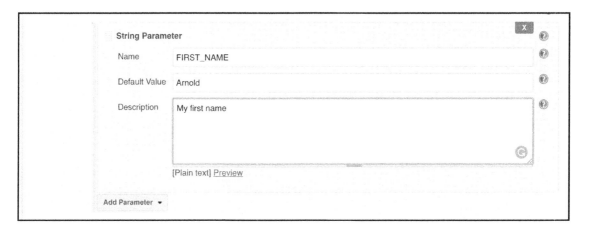

7. Follow the same procedure to create the second parameter for your last name. The final configuration should look like the following screenshot:

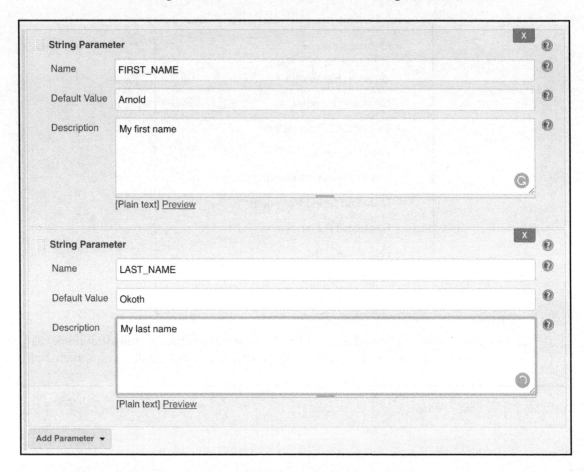

Our project now has two string parameters containing our first and last names. We can now proceed to add the build parameter to display the desired result.

8. In the build section of the project configuration, select the **Add build step** drop-down menu and select **Execute shell**, as shown in the following screenshot:

9. This presents us with a form requiring us to insert the command we want to execute. Populate the text area as shown in the following screenshot:

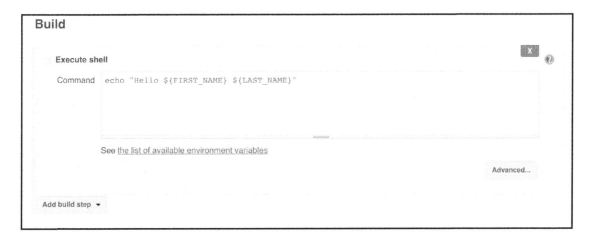

10. Press **Apply** and **Save** at the bottom of the screen to save your project configuration. This will direct you to the project dashboard.

11. On the left-hand project options menu, select **Build with parameters** to build the project:

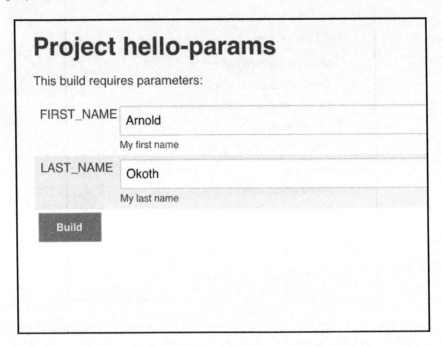

12. Fill in the parameters if you are not comfortable with running the project with the default parameters. Select **Build**.

13. On the build history on the left, hover over the build number and select **Console Output**, as shown in the following screenshot:

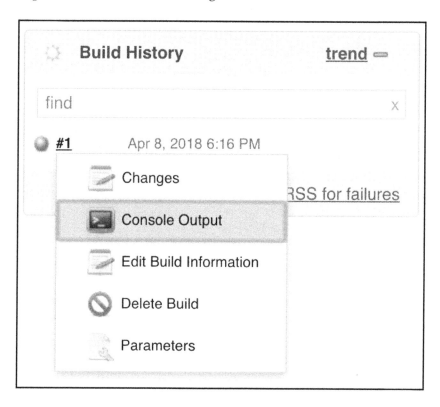

From the **Console Output**, we can see that the build successfully displayed our first and last name, with the greeting as displayed on the following screenshot:

 Console Output

```
Started by user Arnold Okoth
Building on master in workspace /var/lib/jenkins/workspace/hello-params
[hello-params] $ /bin/sh -xe /tmp/jenkins7549596233888412574.sh
+ echo 'Hello Arnold Okoth'
Hello Arnold Okoth
Finished: SUCCESS
```

Build Triggers

While working with Jenkins, there are different ways we can tell Jenkins to run our projects. As seen in the previous chapter, we can run them manually, but while working on real projects, we need more automated ways to run our builds. Build triggers help to make this possible. There are different ways we can achieve this:

- Starting a build job when another job has been completed using upstream/downstream projects
- Running builds at periodic intervals
- Polling source code management for changes
- Triggering builds remotely

In this section, we are going to discuss upstream/downstream projects and, later, use activities to demonstrate the capabilities of other build triggers.

Creating Upstream/Downstream Projects

The first build trigger mechanism mentioned above involves creating two interlinked build tasks. In this section, we will be creating two projects and using one to trigger the other. Given two projects, project A and project B, if project B is configured to run once project A completes, we call project B the downstream project and project A the upstream project. Let's first create `Project A`.

1. Select **New Item** on the Jenkins dashboard and configure it as shown in the following screenshot:

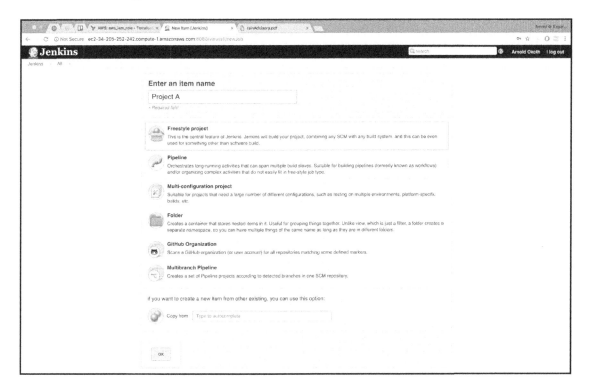

The project build configuration will be very basic, just as we saw in the previous sections.

2. Add a string parameter and a build step to output the parameter, as shown in the following screenshots:

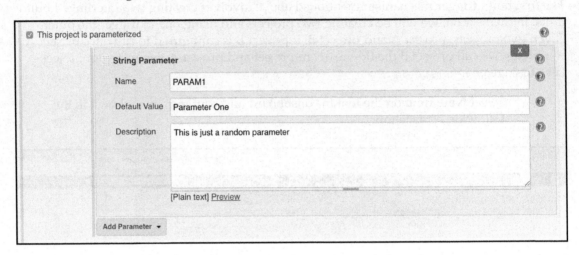

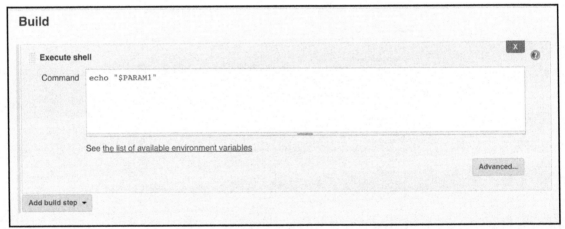

3. Select **Apply** and **Save** at the end of the page.

4. Go back to the dashboard and create `Project B` the same way we set up `Project A`, but with a different parameter identifier.

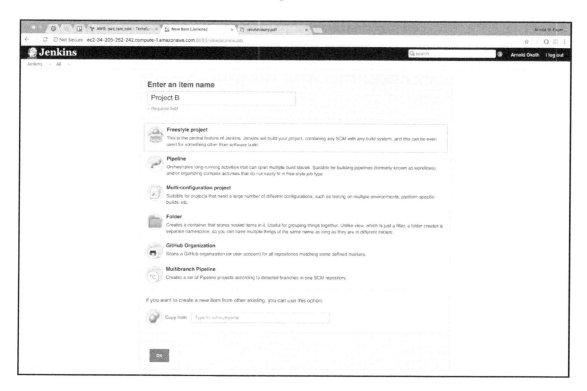

5. Select **OK** to create the project and add the string parameter as follows:

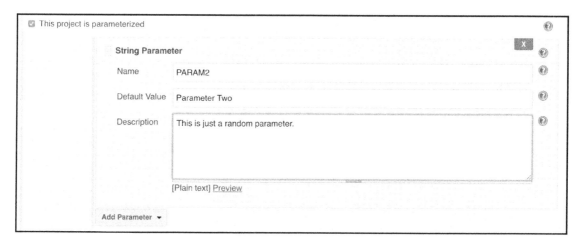

6. Before we add our build step, we have to configure our project as a downstream project. Under **Build Triggers** in the project configuration, select **Build after other projects are built**.

7. After we select the **Build after other projects are built** option, we are presented with a text field in which we have to enter the upstream project, that is, Project A. Start typing the name of the upstream project and Jenkins will autocomplete and filter with the projects that match what you want to specify, as shown in the following screenshot:

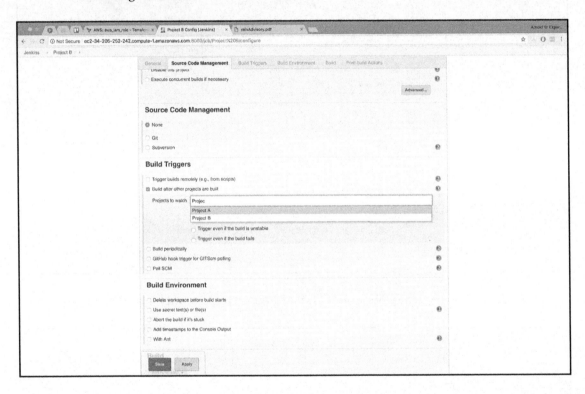

While configuring the upstream project, we can see another list of radio buttons asking us to specify under what conditions we want our downstream project to run:

Trigger only if build is stable will run the downstream project only if the upstream project has successfully run.
Trigger even if the build is unstable will run the downstream project even in if the upstream project is not stable.
Trigger even if the build fails will run the downstream project even if the upstream project fails.

Depending on how you want your builds to interact, you can select the option that best suits your needs, but ideally you will want to run the downstream project only when the upstream project successfully runs and is stable.

8. You can configure multiple upstream projects, thus you will notice a comma after Project A in the **Projects to watch** text field. Your final configuration should look as shown in the following screenshot:

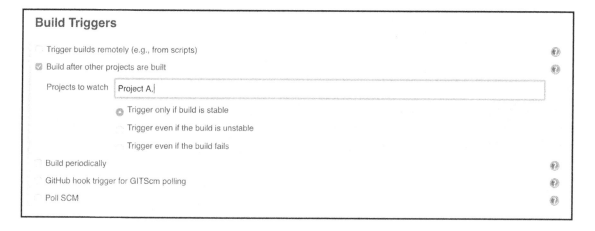

9. Finally, add a build step to execute a shell script that will output the parameter we added earlier, as shown in the following screenshot:

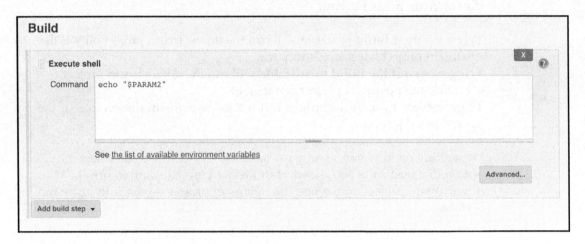

10. Click **Apply** and **Save** to persist the build configuration you just made.

   Before we run our projects, we need to make one more configuration change on our upstream project.

11. While on the Jenkins dashboard, select `Project A`. On the left configuration panel, click on **Configure** and this will open the now familiar project configuration page.

12. Scroll to the bottom to get to the **Post-build Actions** section. Click on **Add post-build action** and select **Build other projects**, as shown in the following screenshot:

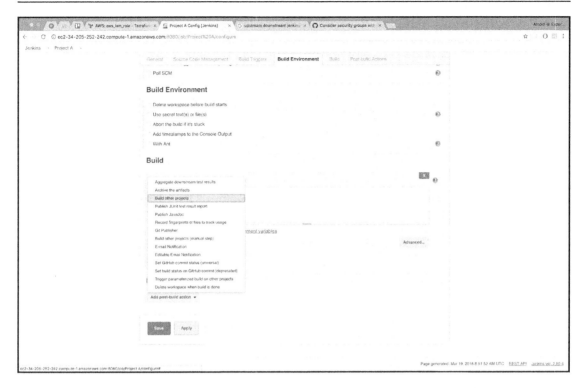

After selecting this, we are presented with a similar prompt to the one we had when configuring the downstream project.

13. Enter `Project B` in **Projects to build** and select the **Trigger only if build is stable** radio button:

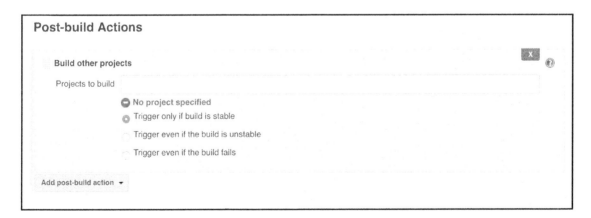

14. Select **Apply** and **Save** to save the configuration.

At this point, we have completed our upstream/downstream configuration.

Running an Upstream Project

Now that we've understood how to configure upstream and downstream projects, let's try to run an upstream project in Jenkins. Follow these steps:

1. Head back to the Jenkins dashboard, click on `Project A`, and, on the left-hand configuration panel, select **Build with parameters**. On the **Build with Parameters** page, click **Build**.

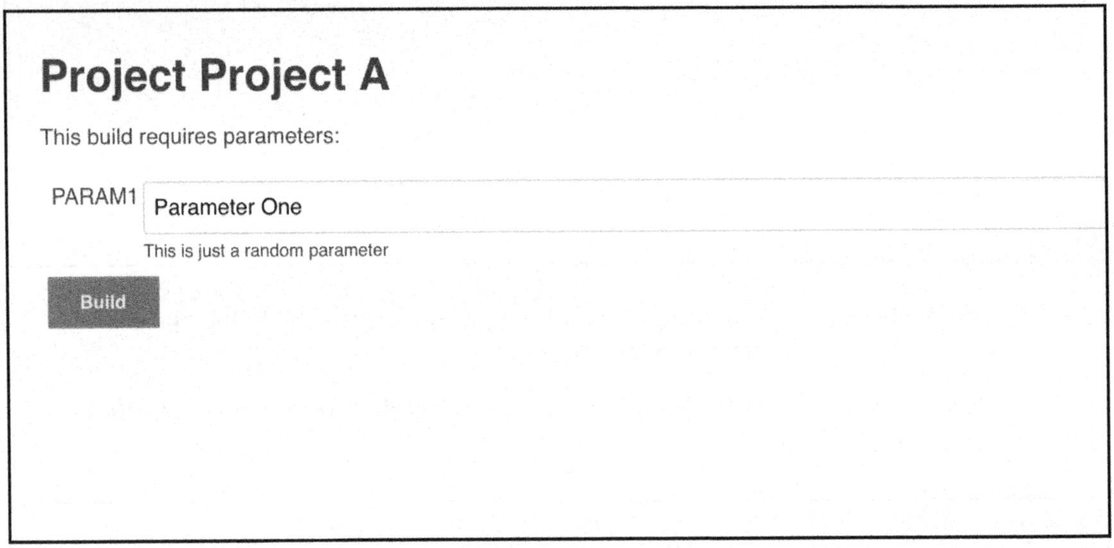

Project Project A

This build requires parameters:

PARAM1 | Parameter One

This is just a random parameter

Build

2. After running the build, we can see it highlights that `Project A` has some downstream projects, as shown in the following screenshot:

3. Select `Project B` under the **Downstream Projects** section. While on `Project B`, go the **Build History** section on the left and hover over the latest build, click the down arrow and select **Console Output**; in this case, that is **#2** (build number 2), as shown in the following screenshot:

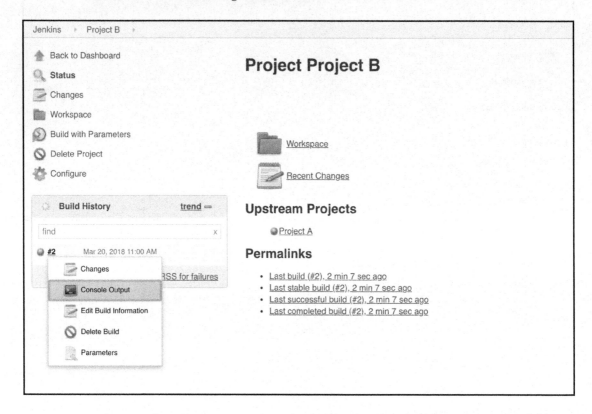

Looking at the output, we can see that the build of `Project B` was triggered by its upstream project. The output also informs us that `Project A` was run by the user.

Console Output

```
Started by upstream project "Project A" build number 2
originally caused by:
 Started by user Arnold Okoth
Started by upstream project "Project A" build number 2
originally caused by:
 Started by user Arnold Okoth
Building in workspace /var/lib/jenkins/workspace/Project B
[Project B] $ /bin/sh -xe /tmp/jenkins8336108615709556622.sh
+ echo 'Parameter Two'
Parameter Two
Finished: SUCCESS
```

Activity: Building a GitHub Project

Scenario

You have been provided with a simple code project on GitHub with test files and have been tasked with creating a Jenkins project that will run the tests in the project.

Aim

To set up a Jenkins version-controlled project to run GitHub test files

Prerequisites

Make sure you have done the following:

- Got Jenkins up and running and have logged in with the appropriate permissions
- Created a GitHub repository with the sample code files
- Created a fork of the GitHub repository and cloned it to your PC

Refer to the complete code files, which have been placed at the following URLs:

Go to `https://bit.ly/2vkaIHh` to access the code for the `sum.py` file.
Go to `https://bit.ly/2L1cTKo` to access the code for the `test_sum.py` file.

Steps for Completion

1. Go to the Jenkins dashboard and, on the configuration panel on the left, select **New Item**.

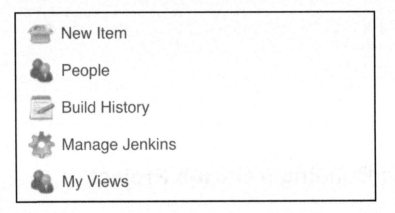

2. Enter an appropriate name for the project, select **Freestyle project**, and select **OK** to save.

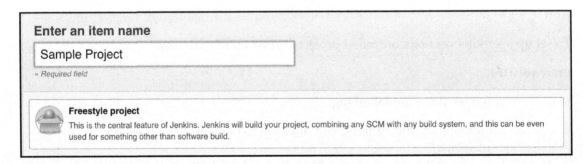

3. Under **Source Code Management** in the project configuration, select the **Git** radio button.

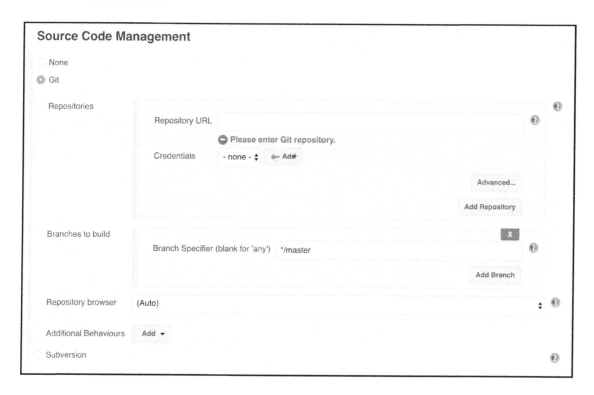

4. Under **Repository URL**, enter the URL of the repository where you have the sample code files. The **Repository URL** is the full URL you get from your browser's URL bar of the location of your code base. Since our repository is public, we will not need to add any credentials; thus, we will leave it as none. Under the branch specifier, we will specify `master`, which will build the master branch upon detecting any new changes.

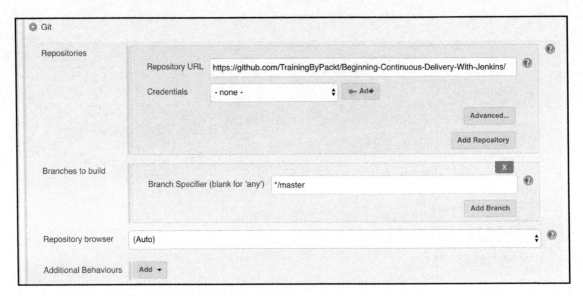

After creating the fork as instructed earlier, the repository URL should be as follows: `https://github.com/<your-profile>/Beginning-Jenkins/`.

5. Finally, add a build step to the project that will execute the shell command to run our tests.

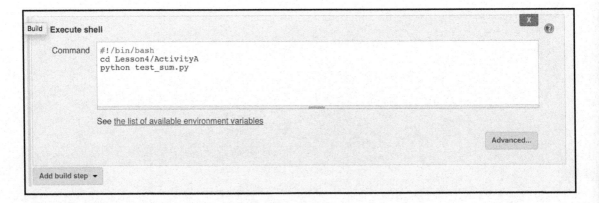

6. Click **Apply** and **Save** to save our project configuration.
7. Open the project dashboard, and select **Build Now**.

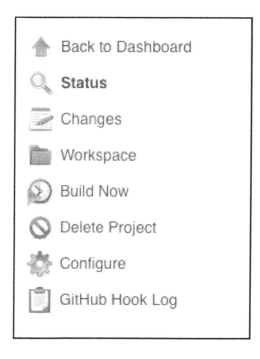

8. Go back to your project dashboard under **Build History**, click on the drop-down menu on the latest build, and select **Console Output**, as shown in the following screenshot:

We can see the output in the following screenshot. The first step just pulls the latest changes from our repository and then our test file is run as the last step, as we specified in the build step.

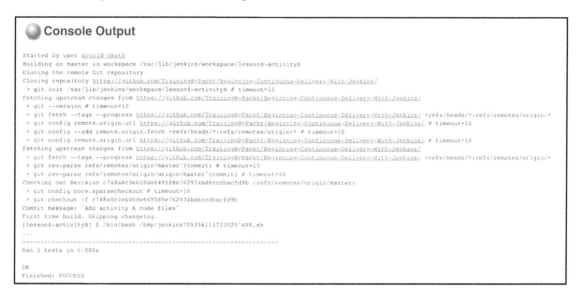

Summary

In this chapter, we learned about build parameters and demonstrated how to configure them. We then demonstrated the importance of build triggers. Lastly, we integrated a sample project with version control and worked with the GitHub build trigger.

In the next chapter, we will delve deeper into identifying Git workflows that enable CI, and demonstrate a version-controlled project with multiple branches.

5
Jenkins Pipelines

In the previous chapters, we managed to cover the following topics:

- Installing and setting up Jenkins on different environments
- Administering and securing Jenkins once installed on our environment
- Creating freestyle projects and customizing the Jenkins interface with views
- Working with parameterized projects and build triggers

In this chapter, we will begin to explore newer features of Jenkins and build a full-on pipeline that will demonstrate the power of CI and automation.

By the end of this chapter, you will be able to:

- Identify Git workflows that enable CI and easily integrate into Jenkins
- Demonstrate a version-controlled project with multiple branches and build it on Jenkins
- Demonstrate how to use the declarative Jenkins pipeline and add your pipeline to version control

The CI Workflow

Before we discuss the CI workflow, it is important to quickly understand the more basic concept of a pipeline in Jenkins. The term **pipeline** is used to refer to a mechanism or a system of moving something, say supplies, from one point to another. In the context of software development, we are referring to shipping an application from development to the end user.

Continuous integration and delivery pipelines help software development to move code from development to different environments such as staging and production. A pipeline provides a fast, repeatable, and consistent process for delivering software. While pipelines vary for different products and scenarios, there are some generic steps that are important on every pipeline. The steps in a CI pipeline depend on the type of project you are running but, at a high level, involve pulling code from source control, preparing a test environment, and running tests. These are mentioned in brief below:

Pulling Code from Source Control: The expectation here is that you have a central repository where every developer regularly checks in code. The pipeline is configured to pull in the latest changes from a centralized repository host such as GitHub or Bitbucket.

Preparing the Application Environment: Depending on the application, this step is optional, but most applications today rely on dependencies that have to be installed prior to running the application. For instance, a Python application could require pip packages, or a Node.js application could have some npm dependencies.

Testing: As mentioned in earlier chapters, test-driven development is a huge enabler of continuous integration; thus, testing is one of the more important stages in a pipeline. This stage will run all the tests in the application and ensure they pass.

Building: Depending on the manner in which the application is shipped or the programming language used, this step may have different configurations, but the result here is a build artifact. A build artifact is a shippable file of your application. If you are using Java, the artifact could potentially be a JAR file, and if you are using Docker, the build artifact will be a Docker image.

Deployment: Depending on the setup, the pipeline may go ahead and deploy the application or wait for some manual input from a member of the team to deploy the application.

Remember the difference between continuous delivery and continuous deployment. Continuous Integration is essentially the practice of conducting your tests on a non-developer system as soon as someone pushes the code into a source repository such as GitHub. This practice helps team members integrate their work in such a way that it is verified by an automated build to identify errors as soon as possible. This results in quicker deployment to production.

This section will take that knowledge further and introduce a branching workflow that will help you set up a CI pipeline.

Git Branches

From the official Git documentation, the term branch is defined as a lightweight movable pointer to a commit. The main branch in Git, by default, is referred to as master and, ideally, this branch should have the most stable code base that is ready for release. As many developers work on a project, the ideal workflow is as follows: one branches off the master (hence the term branch), makes the changes they need, such as adding features and fixing bugs, and then, after they are done, they commit those changes and request a merge back to the master branch, a process referred to on GitHub as making a pull request (PR).

Going back to our definition of a branch, we can see that, as we do this, we are moving this commit pointer outside the main branch so as to not destabilize our code, and once our code is considered worthy or bug-free, it is merged back.

One of the best analogies of branching is one on timelines. Think of a branch as a timeline. The main timeline is the master branch. When we create a branch, we create a new timeline from the master timeline and perform changes to the code base. When we want to merge back to the main timeline, we request a merge and, if our changes did not introduce any bugs or errors, then we are allowed to merge.

 For some of the preceding points, such as code quality and code coverage reports, there are software-as-a-service products, such as Codacy. While some of these features are built into other languages, Golang has a test coverage feature built into the language and no third-party tools are necessary.

We can visualize our workflow as shown in the following diagram:

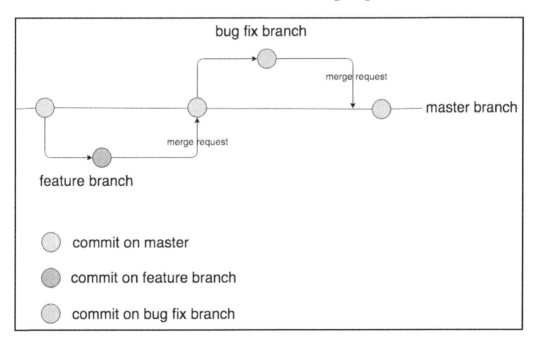

Setting up our Repository

In this section, we will set up our central repository and get a feel of the workflow before we bring it together into a pipeline. This chapter assumes you have a GitHub account. Ensure that you download and install Git from `https://git-scm.com/downloads` before proceeding. Any recently released version of Git should work. To set up a GitHub repository, follow these steps:

1. Navigate to `https://github.com/<your-profile>`.
2. On the top navigation bar, click on the drop-down with a plus sign and select **New repository**, as depicted in the following screenshot:

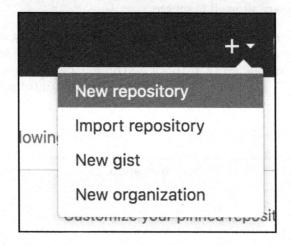

3. Open the new repository form. Configure it as shown in the screenshot and select **Create Repository** at the bottom of the screen:

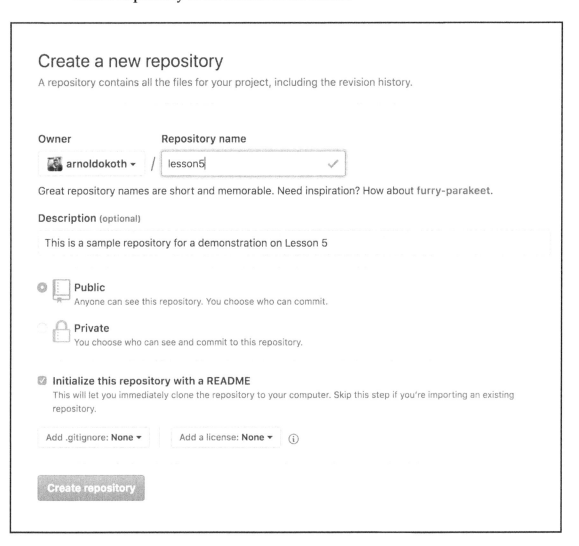

If the repository is successfully created, you will be redirected to the repository page, as follows:

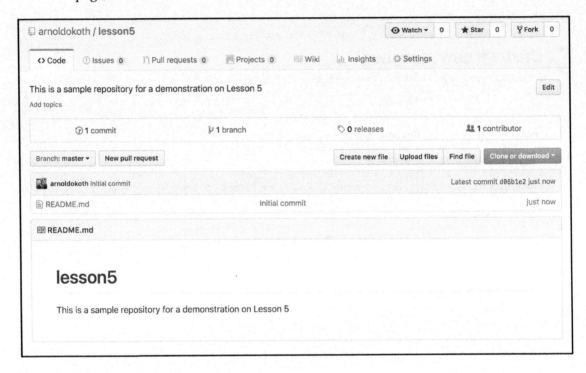

We can see that the name of the repository and the description have been added to the README file.

4. Set up our repository locally. On your command line or Git Bash, create a folder and name it `Lesson5`. Enter the directory as shown:

```
arnoldokoth@Arnolds-MacBook-Pro:~/Projects/Packt
⇒ mkdir Lesson5
arnoldokoth@Arnolds-MacBook-Pro:~/Projects/Packt
⇒ cd Lesson5
arnoldokoth@Arnolds-MacBook-Pro:~/Projects/Packt/Lesson5
⇒ 
```

5. Inside the `Lesson5` folder on your Git bash, run the `git init` command. If the command runs successfully, it should display an output similar to the one displayed in the following screenshot:

```
arnoldokoth@Arnolds-MacBook-Pro:~/Projects/Packt/Lesson5 master
⇒ git remote add origin https://github.com/arnoldokoth/lesson5
arnoldokoth@Arnolds-MacBook-Pro:~/Projects/Packt/Lesson5 master
⇒ 
```

Next, we want to point this local repository to the remote we created on GitHub as the origin.

6. Copy the URL of the repository, which should be:
`https://github.com/<your-profile>/lesson5`. We will use this to run the next command, as follows:

```
arnoldokoth@Arnolds-MacBook-Pro:~/Projects/Packt/Lesson5 master
⇒ git remote add origin https://github.com/arnoldokoth/lesson5
arnoldokoth@Arnolds-MacBook-Pro:~/Projects/Packt/Lesson5 master
⇒ 
```

7. To determine whether we successfully added our remote origin, run the following command:

```
arnoldokoth@Arnolds-MacBook-Pro:~/Projects/Packt/Lesson5|master
⇒ git remote -v
origin  https://github.com/arnoldokoth/lesson5 (fetch)
origin  https://github.com/arnoldokoth/lesson5 (push)
arnoldokoth@Arnolds-MacBook-Pro:~/Projects/Packt/Lesson5|master
⇒
```

From the output, we can see that we successfully added the remote origin as it is listed. Since we initialized our repository with a README on GitHub, we need to pull this to our local repository.

8. Run the following command to pull this to our local repository:

```
arnoldokoth@Arnolds-MacBook-Pro:~/Projects/Packt/Lesson5|master
⇒ git pull origin master
remote: Counting objects: 3, done.
remote: Compressing objects: 100% (2/2), done.
remote: Total 3 (delta 0), reused 0 (delta 0), pack-reused 0
Unpacking objects: 100% (3/3), done.
From https://github.com/arnoldokoth/lesson5
 * branch            master        -> FETCH_HEAD
 * [new branch]      master        -> origin/master
arnoldokoth@Arnolds-MacBook-Pro:~/Projects/Packt/Lesson5|master
⇒
```

If the command runs successfully, we should see an output similar to the one depicted in the above screenshot. This informs us that we have pulled changes from our remote, and if we do a directory listing, we can see that our repository now has a README that only existed on the remote when we began. The output of the ls (directory listing) is depicted here:

```
arnoldokoth@Arnolds-MacBook-Pro:~/Projects/Packt/Lesson5|master
⇒ ls
README.md
arnoldokoth@Arnolds-MacBook-Pro:~/Projects/Packt/Lesson5|master
⇒ █
```

 Before you proceed to the following section, ensure that you have access to Lesson5 code files. There are two files for this section: one contains random functions and the other contains tests for these random functions. Included with the files is a .gitignore that will prevent autogenerated or cached files from getting into your remote repository.

9. Before we add these files, create a new branch called add-functions-and-tests.

10. Use the git checkout command and the –b flag, which will create a new branch if one does not exist.

```
arnoldokoth@Arnolds-MacBook-Pro:~/Projects/Packt/Lesson5|master
⇒ git checkout -b add-functions-and-tests
Switched to a new branch 'add-functions-and-tests'
arnoldokoth@Arnolds-MacBook-Pro:~/Projects/Packt/Lesson5|add-functions-and-tests⚡
⇒ █
```

11. Create the files in the root folder of the project and add them to the Git staging area while on the new branch.

12. Use `git status` to view the files that haven't been tracked, followed by `git add .` to start tracking the files. This process is shown in the following screenshot:

```
arnoldokoth@Arnolds-MacBook-Pro:~/Projects/Packt/Lesson5|add-functions-and-tests ⚡
⇒ git status
On branch add-functions-and-tests
Untracked files:
  (use "git add <file>..." to include in what will be committed)

        .gitignore
        functions.py
        test_functions.py

nothing added to commit but untracked files present (use "git add" to track)
arnoldokoth@Arnolds-MacBook-Pro:~/Projects/Packt/Lesson5|add-functions-and-tests ⚡
⇒ git add .
arnoldokoth@Arnolds-MacBook-Pro:~/Projects/Packt/Lesson5|add-functions-and-tests ⚡
⇒ git status
On branch add-functions-and-tests
Changes to be committed:
  (use "git reset HEAD <file>..." to unstage)

        new file:   .gitignore
        new file:   functions.py
        new file:   test_functions.py

arnoldokoth@Arnolds-MacBook-Pro:~/Projects/Packt/Lesson5|add-functions-and-tests ⚡
⇒ ▌
```

We added the files to the staging area. In the `git add` command, we used a period because we wanted to add all the untracked files in the current folder. At this point, we want to commit our changes and push them to the remote repository. We can achieve this using the `git commit` command flag with the `-m` flag to add a descriptive comment describing our commit. This process is depicted as follows:

```
arnoldokoth@Arnolds-MacBook-Pro:~/Projects/Packt/Lesson5|add-functions-and-tests ⚡
⇒ git commit -m "add functions plus unit tests"
[add-functions-and-tests 41d3908] add functions plus unit tests
 3 files changed, 49 insertions(+)
 create mode 100644 .gitignore
 create mode 100644 functions.py
 create mode 100644 test_functions.py
arnoldokoth@Arnolds-MacBook-Pro:~/Projects/Packt/Lesson5|add-functions-and-tests
⇒ git push origin add-functions-and-tests
Counting objects: 5, done.
Delta compression using up to 4 threads.
Compressing objects: 100% (4/4), done.
Writing objects: 100% (5/5), 837 bytes | 837.00 KiB/s, done.
Total 5 (delta 0), reused 0 (delta 0)
To https://github.com/arnoldokoth/lesson5
 * [new branch]        add-functions-and-tests -> add-functions-and-tests
arnoldokoth@Arnolds-MacBook-Pro:~/Projects/Packt/Lesson5|add-functions-and-tests
⇒
```

Going back to our project dashboard on GitHub, we can see that a new branch has been added:

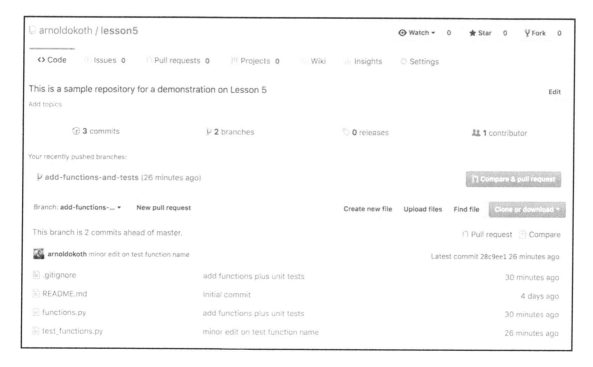

Let's create a pull request to our master branch, allowing us to merge the changes from our new branch.

13. Select the **Compare & pull request** button to create and configure our pull request:

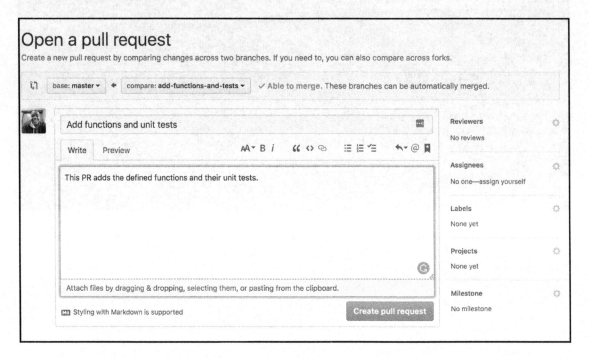

The base branch is the branch you want to merge to, and the compare branch is the branch you want to merge. We will then press the **Create pull request** button to create our pull request. This lands us on the pull request page, where we can see a few more things regarding our project. Of most importance is the output in the **Merge pull request section**:

GitHub informs us that CI has not been set up. Before a **Pull Request** is considered mergeable, GitHub will ensure all integrated checks have certified the PR. This includes what we mentioned earlier, that is testing, linting, and so on.

Creating a GitHub Repository and Integrating Jenkins

Let's say that you have been tasked with setting up a new GitHub repository and adding Jenkins service integration (you can use the same code files that were provided earlier in this section). Ensure that you have Jenkins up and running, and that you are authenticated as the admin. To create a pipeline project by integrating Jenkins with a GitHub repository, follow these steps:

1. Go to the GitHub dashboard and create a new repository.
2. On the repository configuration page, initialize the project with a README file.
3. Create a folder locally and initialize it using the `git init` command.
4. Add a remote named `origin` and point it to the GitHub repository you just created.
5. Pull changes from the remote repository to your local repository.
6. Checkout to a new branch called `add-code-files`. Add the provided code samples to your project while under this branch and push the changes to the remote repository.
7. Create a pull request from your new branch to the base branch of master.

8. Go to the repository settings and add the Jenkins GitHub plugin integration. This is under **Settings** -> **Webhooks**.

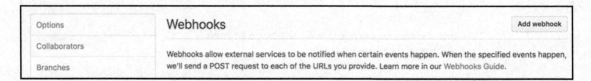

9. Click on the **Add webhook** button at the top. This will present you with the following form:

Webhooks / **Add webhook**

We'll send a POST request to the URL below with details of any subscribed events. You can also specify which data format you'd like to receive (JSON, x-www-form-urlencoded, *etc*). More information can be found in our developer documentation.

Payload URL *

> https://example.com/postreceive

Content type

> application/x-www-form-urlencoded ⬍

Secret

Which events would you like to trigger this webhook?

🔘 Just the push event.

◯ Send me **everything**.

◯ Let me select individual events.

☑ **Active**
We will deliver event details when this hook is triggered.

Add webhook

For the Payload URL, enter your DNS entry for your hosted Jenkins instance followed by `/github-webhook/`, for example, `http://your-jenkins-url/github-webhook/`. Leave the rest of the form fields as they are and trigger the webhook using **Just the push event**.

After successful integration of the Jenkins service, you should see it listed as shown below. Note the green tick on the left, which verifies that the integration works as expected.

The webhook configuration only works with a hosted Jenkins setup. Alternatively, you can start builds manually, depending on the project type:

- For a pipeline project, go to the project dashboard and select **Build Now** from the left-hand side menu.

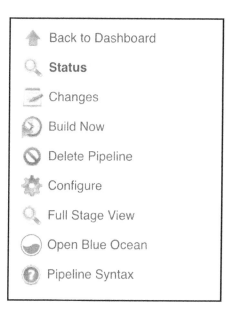

- For a multibranch pipeline project, which will be presented in the last topic of this section, select **Scan Repository Now** from the left-hand side menu.

In the next section, we will build upon this exercise and create a pipeline for it with Jenkins.

The Jenkinsfile

A pipeline in Jenkins is defined using a script called the **Jenkinsfile**. This provides more automation, allows your pipeline to be treated like all other application code, and can be stored in version control. This provides more benefits for your team since your pipeline can be reviewed like code and the pipeline acts as a single source of truth. In this section, we will cover the two ways of creating the pipeline, from the web UI and by adding it to source control. We will also learn how to configure Jenkins to read from the remote repository.

The pipeline syntax can be presented in two forms: **declarative** and **scripted**. The declarative syntax is a simple and opinionated way of writing your pipeline. The scripted pipeline is built with Groovy and is generally a more flexible and expressive way of creating your pipelines. When choosing which model to use, it all depends on your requirements. The declarative model works with simple pipelines and lacks most of the flexibility offered by the scripted model. We will be working with the scripted pipeline in this chapter.

In the previous section, we learned about the branching workflow, which enables us to make the most out of our CI setup and makes it easier for our teams to collaborate on a project. In this section, we will create the pipeline script for our project with the necessary steps required for it to run.

While working with the Jenkins scripted pipeline, we use standard Groovy syntax. The scripted pipeline has some special directives that perform different functions. Let's explain each directive we see in our pipeline script:

Directive	Explanation node
`node`	This defines where the job is going to be run. We will explore more about this in the next chapter as we cover setting up master-slave relationships on Jenkins.
`dir`	This directive defines what directory/folder to run the following directives on.
`stage`	This defines the stage of your pipeline, for example, what task it's running.
`git`	This points to the remote repository where you pull the changes from.
`sh`	This defines the shell script to run on a UNIX-based environment. On a Windows environment, we would use the `bat` directive instead.
`def`	As mentioned previously, the pipeline is written in Groovy; thus, we can define functions to perform different actions. In this case, we defined a `printMessage` function, which prints out different messages at the start and end of our pipeline.

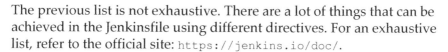

The previous list is not exhaustive. There are a lot of things that can be achieved in the Jenkinsfile using different directives. For an exhaustive list, refer to the official site: `https://jenkins.io/doc/`.

Also, note the different kinds of pipelines, that is, declarative versus scripted. Both of these have different syntax and they are not compatible. So, while viewing the documentation, be careful not to use the declarative syntax while working with a scripted pipeline and vice versa.

Creating the Pipeline

In the previous section, we created a project and added sample code files plus some unit tests. However, we never integrated our project into Jenkins to confirm that our code actually works. We will create a pipeline in this section, adding a few basic stages to it to run our tests.

1. Go to the Jenkins dashboard and select **New Item**.
2. Enter an appropriate name for the project and select **Pipeline** for the project type.
3. In the project configuration, under the **General** tab, select **GitHub project** and enter the appropriate URL.

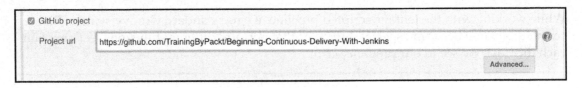

4. Under the **Build Triggers** section, select the **GitHub hook trigger for GITScm polling**, which will help us automatically trigger builds on our pipeline whenever a commit is pushed to GitHub. This configuration will only work with a hosted Jenkins server and configured GitHub webhook on the repository.

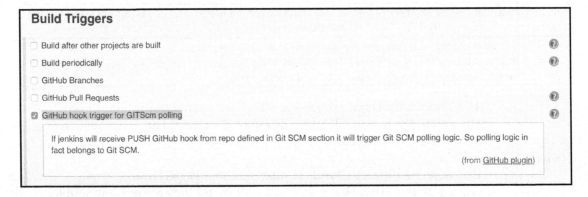

The final configuration of the project is creating our pipeline.

5. Under the pipeline section, select **Pipeline script** under **Definition**.

Pipeline

Definition	Pipeline script	⬍

6. In the script section of the configuration, add the following snippet of code:

```
1   node('master') {
2       stage("Fetch Source Code") {
3           git 'https://github.com/TrainingByPackt/Beginning-Continuous-Delivery-With-Jenkins'
4       }
5
6       dir('Lesson5') {
7           printMessage('Running Pipeline')
8
9           stage("Testing") {
10              sh 'python test_functions.py'
11          }
12
13          printMessage('Pipeline Complete')
14      }
15  }
16
17  def printMessage(message) {
18      echo "${message}"
19  }
20
```

Your final pipeline script configuration should look like this:

Pipeline

Definition	Pipeline script	⬍

```
Script        1 ▾ node('master') {
              2 ▾     stage("Fetch Source Code") {
              3            git 'https://github.com/TrainingByPackt/Beginning-Continuous-Delivery-With-Jenk
              4        }
              5
              6 ▾     dir('Lesson5') {
              7            printMessage('Running Pipeline')
              8
              9 ▾         stage("Testing") {
             10                sh 'python test_functions.py'
             11            }
             12
             13            printMessage('Pipeline Complete')
             14        }
             15 }
             16
```

☑ Use Groovy Sandbox

Pipeline Syntax

7. Press **Apply** to save the configuration so far before Jenkins logs you out, which may result in some data loss.

8. Select **Save** to persist your configuration and redirect you back to the project dashboard.

9. Select **Build Now** on the left-hand menu to build your project. Since we have no commits to push, we will manually trigger a build.

10. On the project dashboard, after running our build, the **Stage View** shows up.

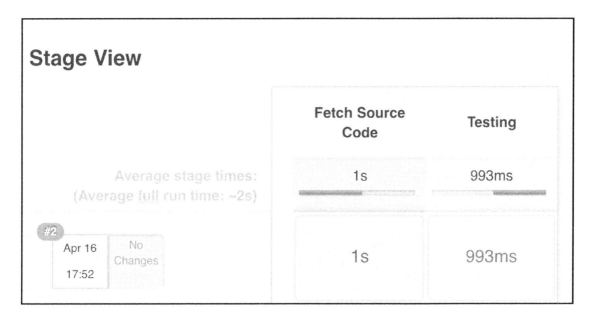

We can see the stages we configured earlier on in our pipeline and the amount of time it took to run each step. By hovering over and clicking each time length, we can view the logs and exactly which commands ran for that stage. For instance, the output for the first stage is as follows:

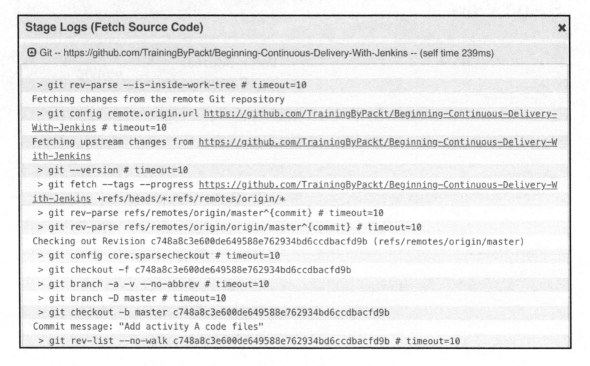

Stage Logs (Fetch Source Code)

```
○ Git -- https://github.com/TrainingByPackt/Beginning-Continuous-Delivery-With-Jenkins -- (self time 239ms)

 > git rev-parse --is-inside-work-tree # timeout=10
Fetching changes from the remote Git repository
 > git config remote.origin.url https://github.com/TrainingByPackt/Beginning-Continuous-Delivery-
With-Jenkins # timeout=10
Fetching upstream changes from https://github.com/TrainingByPackt/Beginning-Continuous-Delivery-W
ith-Jenkins
 > git --version # timeout=10
 > git fetch --tags --progress https://github.com/TrainingByPackt/Beginning-Continuous-Delivery-W
ith-Jenkins +refs/heads/*:refs/remotes/origin/*
 > git rev-parse refs/remotes/origin/master^{commit} # timeout=10
 > git rev-parse refs/remotes/origin/origin/master^{commit} # timeout=10
Checking out Revision c748a8c3e600de649588e762934bd6ccdbacfd9b (refs/remotes/origin/master)
 > git config core.sparsecheckout # timeout=10
 > git checkout -f c748a8c3e600de649588e762934bd6ccdbacfd9b
 > git branch -a -v --no-abbrev # timeout=10
 > git branch -D master # timeout=10
 > git checkout -b master c748a8c3e600de649588e762934bd6ccdbacfd9b
Commit message: "Add activity A code files"
 > git rev-list --no-walk c748a8c3e600de649588e762934bd6ccdbacfd9b # timeout=10
```

Installing Blue Ocean

While this is awesome, Jenkins has a new way of visualizing pipelines, called **Blue Ocean**. We will install Blue Ocean from the plugin manager since it is packaged as a plugin.

Be sure to confirm that the version of Jenkins you are working with is compatible with Blue Ocean. Remember from our chapter on managing plugins that not all plugins are compatible with all versions of Jenkins. Blue Ocean plays well with newer versions of Jenkins in particular.

1. On the Jenkins home dashboard, go to **Manage Jenkins** -> **Manage Plugins**. Under the **Available** tab, search for Blue Ocean.

2. Select **Blue Ocean** and click **Install without restart** at the bottom of the page.

3. On the installation page, select **Restart Jenkins when installation is complete and no jobs are running**.

While restarting Jenkins is not necessary, it is highly recommended. Some plugins might misbehave when installed without a restart. In order to avoid this, restart Jenkins when you install a plugin, but do this during scheduled maintenance periods or select the option on Jenkins to wait for running builds to complete before performing a restart. You can also restart Jenkins using `http://<base_url>/safeRestart`.

4. After successfully installing and restarting Jenkins, when we go back to the Jenkins main dashboard, we see that a new item has been added to our configuration panel on the left, called **Open Blue Ocean**.

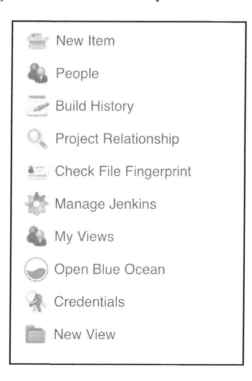

The Blue Ocean dashboard will display your project on your Jenkins server. We will focus on the project we just created in this chapter. In this case, it is called `lesson5-pipeline` and its dashboard is depicted in the following screenshot:

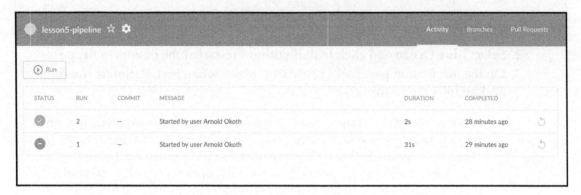

5. Select the latest build, which in this case is build 2. We can also see the pipeline view in an intuitive way, as follows:

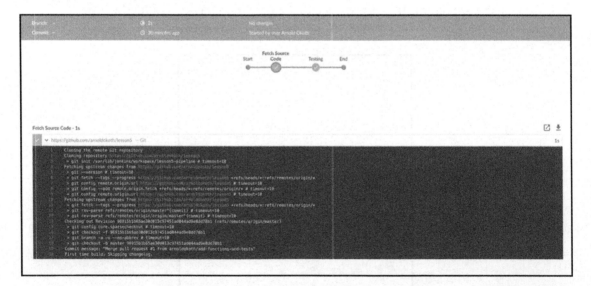

Selecting any stage reveals the steps that ran under each of them. We can also view the console output easily by selecting a stage and then clicking the drop-down next to each command run at that stage.

Creating Multibranch Pipelines

While working on a multibranch project, multibranch pipelines will enable you to build different branches besides the default. As we are going to see in this section, these pipelines provide more flexibility by allowing you to perform different actions on different branches and to perform builds on merge requests.

Global Variables

A variable is a name associated to a value. A global variable is accessible in any scope within our program and is not bound to any scope, such as a function.

While working with the scripted Jenkins pipeline, we can configure it to work with different branches. There are pre-defined global variables available on Jenkins that allow us to use conditionals to perform different actions. For instance, there is a BRANCH_NAME global variable, which allows you to perform different actions, such as deploying while building the master branch, as opposed to while building a feature or bug branch. In this section, we'll learn how to set up global variables and create a multibranch pipeline in Jenkins.

1. To view the global variable reference, go to the pipeline project configuration page.
2. Go to the text area where you entered the pipeline script.
3. Click on the hyperlink labelled **Pipeline Syntax**.

```
11
12        printMessage('Pipeline Complete')
13    }
14
15 ▾ def printMessage(message) {
```

☑ Use Groovy Sandbox

Pipeline Syntax

4. This will land you on the **Pipeline Syntax** page.

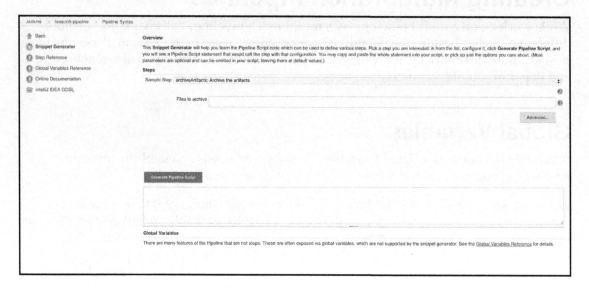

This page serves as documentation and a quick reference while working with pipelines. There is a snippet generator that helps you while working with the scripted pipeline to generate different portions of the pipeline. This is very important as a remembering aid since some pipeline steps have complicated syntax that might be difficult to master.

5. On the left-hand menu, open the **Global Variable Reference** item. This opens the reference page, entailing a global variable reference that would take a while to go through. In our case, we are looking for the BRANCH_NAME variable. We can find this under the env section. The following output displays a portion of the variables:

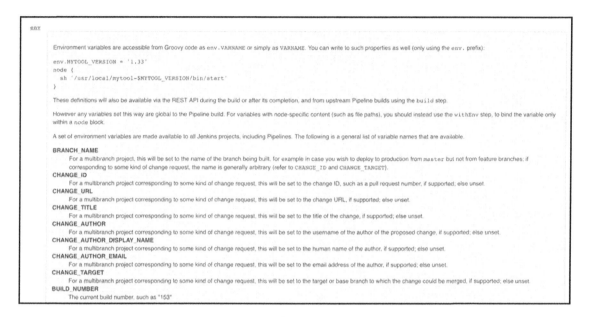

The first variable is the BRANCH_NAME; this is followed by a short description of exactly what it does and how it can be used. We will add a conditional to our pipeline that will just print out a message that our application is being deployed when building the master branch.

Refer to the complete code, which has been placed at https://bit.ly/2KWNgug.

6. Add the following updated script to your pipeline after the testing stage to create a new multibranch project, and add our Jenkinsfile to version control. The final script looks as follows:

```
1   node('master') {
2       stage("Fetch Source Code") {
3           git 'https://github.com/TrainingByPackt/Beginning-Continuous-Delivery-With-Jenkins'
4       }
5
6       dir('Lesson5') {
7           printMessage('Running Pipeline')
8
9           stage("Testing") {
10              sh 'python test_functions.py'
11          }
12
13          stage("Deployment") {
14              if (env.BRANCH_NAME == 'master') {
15                  printMessage('Deploying the master branch')
16              } else {
17                  printMessage('No deployment configured for this branch')
18              }
19          }
20
21          printMessage('Pipeline Complete')
22      }
23  }
24
25  def printMessage(message) {
26      echo "${message}"
27  }
28
```

7. Create this script, add it to the root folder of your project while on the master branch, and name it Jenkinsfile. This Jenkinsfile is located in the Lesson5 folder on the GitHub repository.

8. Add this script to the staging area, create a commit, and push it to the GitHub repository.

9. Create a new project on Jenkins and, under the Project type, select **Multibranch pipeline** and enter an appropriate name for the project.

10. Under **Branch Sources**, select **Add source** and select **GitHub**, as follows.

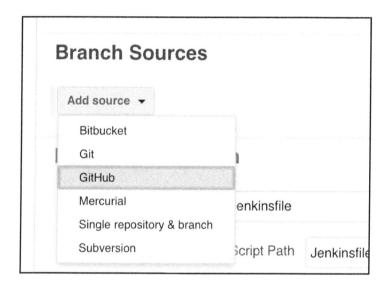

This will pop up a configuration form asking us for the origin repository. Configure the form, filling in **Owner** with your GitHub username or the username of where the repository is hosted, and **Repository** with the name of the repository. Leave the rest as defaults, just like in the following screenshot:

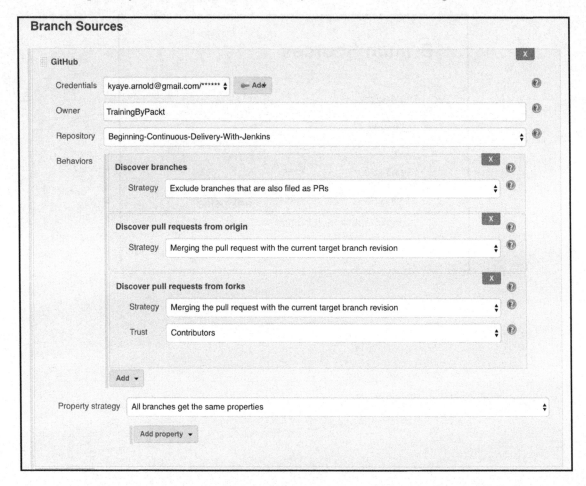

As we can see from the **Credentials** section, there is a warning informing us that adding credentials is recommended. We'll need to add GitHub credentials.

11. Select **Add Dropdown** and select **Jenkins**, as shown:

12. Under **Kind**, select **Username with password**.

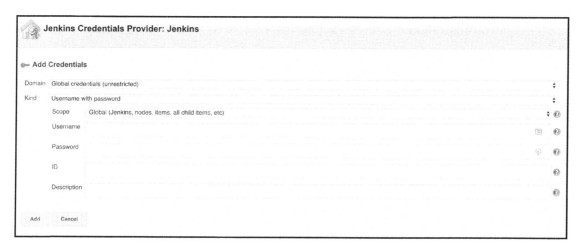

13. Enter your GitHub username and password in their respective fields and select **Add**.

The ID will be automatically generated by Jenkins, and the description is optional.

14. Back on the project configuration page, select the credentials you just created under the **Credentials** section.

We mentioned the importance of the question mark icon in an earlier section. You can use this icon at this point to discover more about the rest of the configurations under the **Behaviors** section.

15. Under the **Build Configuration** section, set up the project as shown.

This configuration informs Jenkins where to find the `Jenkinsfile` we added to our project earlier, which in our case is in the root folder of our project. The rest of the configuration is not relevant for this project, so we can leave it as is.

16. Select **Apply** and **Save** to persist the configuration. Going back to the project dashboard, we can see that our pipeline already ran against the master branch.

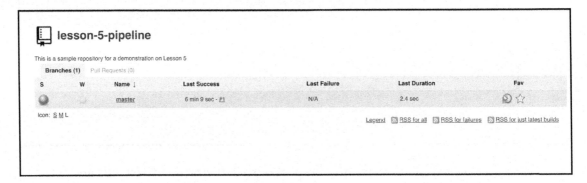

17. On the left-hand panel, select **Open Blue Ocean**. Under the **Branches** tab, select the first item, which in our case is **master**. We will view this project using Blue Ocean as follows:

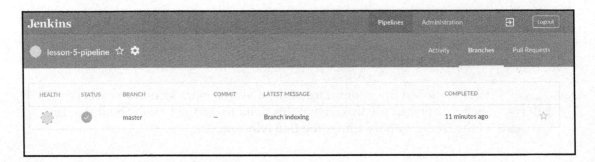

From the output, we can see that our pipeline ran and added the new stage we defined in our script.

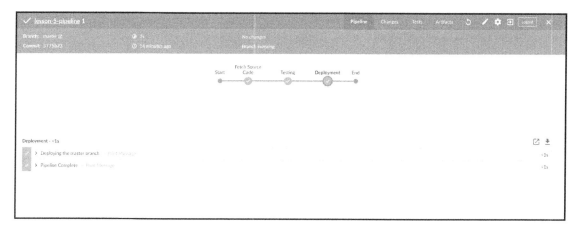

Looking closely at the deployment stage output, we can see that the deployment message that we configured for the master branch, **Deploying the master branch**, was displayed.

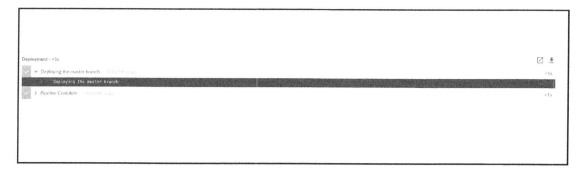

Building Pull Requests

Now that we've covered how to create multibranch projects, we will add a new branch to our project, as well as some functions and tests, and then push our branch to the remote repository. To build pull requests using Jenkins, follow these steps:

1. On your Git Bash in the project root, check out to a new branch and add the following snippet to the `functions.py` file.

```
22  def get_full_name(firstname, lastname):
23      """ Return the full name in the format firstname, lastname
24
25      Arguments:
26      firstname: First name e.g. John
27      lastname: Last name e.g. Doe
28      """
29      return lastname + ", " + firstname
30
```

 This snippet is located in the `Lesson5/functions.py` file. You can copy and paste it directly from this file. Refer to the complete code, which has been placed at `https://bit.ly/2uqgwiI`.

2. In the `test_functions.py` file, add the following unit test for the new function we just added.

```
def test_full_name(self):
    self.assertEqual("Doe, John", get_full_name("John", "Doe"))
```

 This file is already provided in the GitHub repository, under `Lesson5/test_functions.py`. Refer to the complete code, which has been placed at `https://bit.ly/2KYKOmZ`.

Optionally, you can run this test locally (if you have Python installed) to make sure that everything works by using python `test_functions.py`. This is also highlighted in the pipeline script.

3. Once the tests are okay, push the new branch to the remote and create a new pull request.

4. Going back to Jenkins, we can see our new branch and, under the **Pull Requests** tab, we can see that the Pull Request we created has been built by Jenkins using the same pipeline stages.

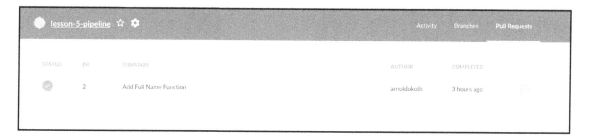

We can view the output of the build. Digging deeper into the Deployment stage, we can see from the output that no deployment was configured for the branch that ran as a result of the conditional we configured earlier.

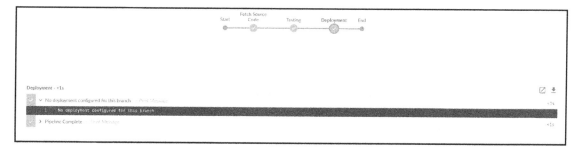

At this point, we have managed to create an end-to-end pipeline with GitHub merge checks integrated. If any of the pipeline stages failed, GitHub would report the branch as not mergeable since there are errors in the pipeline.

Activity: Creating a Pipeline

Scenario

You have been provided with a Python code base with test files and custom requirements that the application depends on, and have been tasked with creating a Jenkins pipeline script that will run the tests and perform a mock deployment against the master branch, which will just print a message that the master branch is getting deployed on the console.

Aim

To get familiar with the GitHub build trigger and integrating a version-controlled project into Jenkins

Steps for Completion

1. Log in to GitHub and open the following URL: `https://github.com/ TrainingByPackt/Beginning-Jenkins/tree/master/Lesson5/ActivityA`.
2. Create a fork of this repository to your account. You can perform this using the **Fork** button at the top right of the screen below the navigation bar.
3. After performing a fork, clone the repository (the fork that is now under your account) to your local machine. We can achieve this by using the `git clone <repo-url>` command.
4. Open the repository in a code editor of your choice.
5. Navigate to the `Lesson5/ActivityA` directory. Looking at the code base as it is right now, it has the following files:

```
.
├── Jenkinsfile.outline
├── Makefile
├── README.md
├── app
│   ├── app.py
│   └── tests
│       └── test_endpoints.py
└── requirements.txt
```

6. Create a Jenkinsfile (pipeline script) from the provided template. On the root folder, we will create a Jenkinsfile and copy over the contents of the template to the Jenkinsfile.

 Refer to the complete code, which has been placed at `https://bit.ly/2JsE37w`.

After performing this operation, the folder structure will look as follows:

```
.
├── Jenkinsfile
├── Jenkinsfile.outline
├── Makefile
├── README.md
├── app
│   ├── app.py
│   └── tests
│       └── test_endpoints.py
└── requirements.txt
```

Opening our newly created Jenkinsfile, we can see the following code inside it:

```
1   node {
2       printMessage("Pipeline Start")
3
4       stage("Fetch Source Code") {
5           git 'https://github.com/<your-profile>/Beginning-Continuous-Delivery-With-Jenkins'
6       }
7
8       dir('Lesson5/ActivityA') {
9           stage("Install Requirements") {
10              sh '<enter makefile command to install requirements>'
11          }
12
13          stage("Run Tests") {
14              sh '<enter makefile command to run tests>'
15          }
16
17          stage("Deploy") {
18              if (env.BRANCH_NAME == "master") {
19                  printMessage("")
20              } else {
21                  printMessage("")
22              }
23          }
24      }
25
26      printMessage("Pipeline End")
27  }
28
29  def printMessage(message) {
30      echo "${message}"
31  }
32
```

7. Make changes to this script and replace the parts enclosed in angle brackets <>
   with the appropriate commands/values (this also includes the angle brackets, as
   depicted in the previous screenshot).

Refer to the complete code, which has been placed at https://bit.ly/
2LcXhD6.

For the first stage, which in our case is **Fetch Source Code**, enter the URL for the forked repository, which is the repository that is now under your account:

```
stage("Fetch Source Code") {
    git "https://github.com/<your-profile>/Beginning-Continuous-Delivery-With-Jenkins|"
}
```

8. For the next stage, add the command listed in the **Makefile** that runs the tests. Our **Makefile** is very basic and has the following tasks:

```
M  Makefile  ✕

1    install:
2        virtualenv testing
3        . testing/bin/activate
4        pip install --user -r requirements.txt
5
6    jenkins_test:
7        testing/bin/nosetests app/ -v
8    |
```

The first task creates a virtual environment (since we are working with Python, this creates a virtual environment for our tests to run in) and installs the project requirements using `pip`. `pip` is a Python package manager similar to `npm` for Node.js. Our requirements are listed in the `requirements.txt` file. The second task runs our tests using the `nosetests` test runner.

 Refer to the complete code, which has been placed at `https://bit.ly/2Nh3taE`.

9. For the **Install Requirements** stage, replace the text enclosed in angle brackets with the `make install` command. The final result should look as follows:

```
stage("Install Requirements") {
    sh 'make install'
}
```

10. Repeat this step but for the **Run Tests** stage, this time replacing the text with the `jenkins_test` command.

11. For the last stage, which in our case is the **Deploy** stage, we will just print appropriate messages for the conditional we currently have in our pipeline script. The final result should look something like the following:

```
stage("Deploy") {
    if (env.BRANCH_NAME == "master") {
        printMessage("deploying master branch")
    } else {
        printMessage("no deployment specified for this branch")
    }
}
```

At this point, we are done updating our pipeline script and need to push it to the remote repository. Push the changes you made to the remote repository.

12. Go to the Jenkins dashboard and create a project, give it an appropriate name, and select the **Multibranch pipeline** on the project type.

13. On the project configuration, under **Branch Sources**, add the repository under your account. For the credentials, you can reuse the ones we created earlier in this chapter. The final **Branch Sources** configuration should look similar to that in the following screenshot:

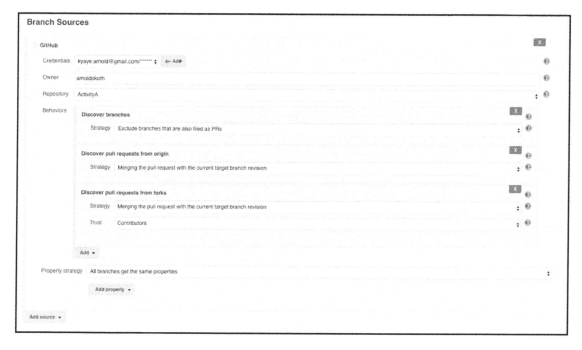

Leave the **Build Configuration** as default. The **Mode** should be **by Jenkinsfile** and the Script Path should be **Jenkinsfile**.

14. Click **Apply** and **Save** to save the pipeline project and open the Blue Ocean dashboard.

If the GitHub webhook was configured correctly, Jenkins will perform a build on the master branch and run the stages that you configured on the pipeline script. Start the build manually by clicking on the play button as follows:

Summary

In this chapter, we have learned about branching with Git and how this enables a CI workflow. We then demonstrated working with the Jenkinsfile and how to create pipelines for our projects hosted on GitHub. Lastly, we created a multibranch pipeline and demonstrated how to configure our pipeline to perform different actions while building different branches. In the next chapter, we are going to cover how to set up distributed builds on Jenkins and how to configure our projects to run on our agents, thus creating a faster build environment

Distributed Builds on Jenkins 6

In the previous chapters, we managed to cover the following topics:

- Installing and setting up Jenkins on different environments
- Administering and securing Jenkins once installed on our environment
- Creating freestyle projects and customizing the Jenkins interface with views
- Working with parameterized projects and build triggers
- Creating pipelines on Jenkins with different stages

In this chapter, we will begin to explore how we can offload builds from our primary Jenkins server, improve build speeds, and horizontally scale our Jenkins server.

By the end of this chapter, you will be able to:

- Connect agents to your Jenkins master and access them securely
- Configure freestyle projects to run on your agents
- Instruct pipelines to run on different agents in your build environment

Setting up our Slaves

Before we discuss setting up the slaves, it is important to quickly understand the more basic concept of **distributed builds** in Jenkins.

Distributed Builds

In computing, the term distributed is used to refer to a system made up of different components that communicate over a network and pass messages and instructions to each other. Different components of the system are set up on different servers on the same network, ideally for faster communication. In the context of Jenkins, distributed builds refers to the allocation of different nodes (slaves) to run your build tasks. On the flip side, we can also see that the creation of more nodes is expensive and could present a security challenge, since your nodes have to communicate over a network.

The Master-Slave Model

The master-slave model allows us to configure distributed builds on Jenkins. The master node is basically the node on which Jenkins is installed. This is the administrative node that carries out most of the tasks for your build system. Each node on Jenkins has executors by default. The master has two build executors.

The official Jenkins documentation defines an executor as "a slot for execution of work defined by a Pipeline or Project on a Node. A Node may have zero or more Executors configured, which corresponds to how many concurrent Projects or Pipelines are able to execute on that Node."

We can think of an executor as a process that Jenkins starts on a node to execute a task or a build. While setting up slave nodes, you can configure the number of executors for that node. Ideally, the resources (RAM, CPU, and so on) should guide you regarding how many executors you can configure for the slave nodes so that you don't overwhelm the node. Some setups take it a step further and entirely offload the master from running any tasks by setting its executors to 0, but this is not necessarily recommended as it might create long build queues in instances where your master cannot communicate with the slaves.

In this chapter, we will make use of Vagrant and VirtualBox to create a network and a master and slave setup for our Jenkins setup. The code files for this section are provided with this book. These tools are cross-platform and should work on any environment. Assuming you have Vagrant and VirtualBox installed, run `vagrant --version` to confirm that your installation worked fine. At the time of writing this book, the latest Vagrant version is 2.1.1:

```
→ Lesson6 git:(master) ✗ vagrant --version
Vagrant 2.1.1
```

Before you proceed, also ensure that you have a Vagrant Cloud account and that you have run it on your terminal before proceeding. If you have already done this, you can run `vagrant login --check` to confirm that your login session is still active.

The setup we are going to provision is depicted in the following network diagram:

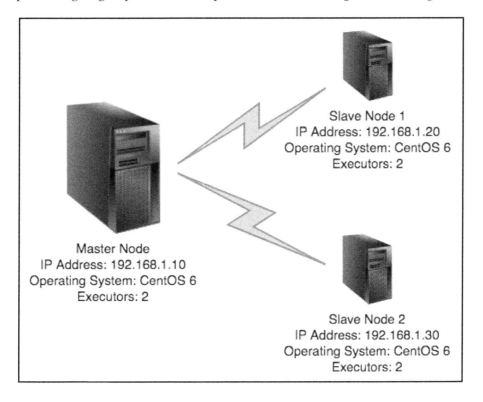

Setting up our Nodes

For this section, we have provided a Vagrantfile. This file describes the type of machines required for this project and how to provision the machines. The file is depicted as follows:

```ruby
# -*- mode: ruby -*-
# vi: set ft=ruby :

# All Vagrant configuration is done below. The "2" in Vagrant.configure
# configures the configuration version (we support older styles for
# backwards compatibility). Please don't change it unless you know what
# you're doing.
Vagrant.configure("2") do |config|
  # Jenkins Master Server
  config.vm.define "master" do |master|
    master.vm.box = "nrel/CentOS-6.5-x86_64"
    master.vm.hostname = "master"
    master.vm.network "private_network", ip: "192.168.1.10"
    master.vm.network "forwarded_port", guest: 8080, host: 8080
    master.vm.provision "shell", path: "provision_master.sh"
  end

  # Slave Node 1
  config.vm.define "node1" do |node1|
    node1.vm.box = "nrel/CentOS-6.5-x86_64"
    node1.vm.hostname = "node1"
    node1.vm.network "private_network", ip: "192.168.1.20"
    node1.vm.provision "shell", path: "provision_slave.sh"
  end

  # Slave Node 2
  config.vm.define "node2" do |node2|
    node2.vm.box = "nrel/CentOS-6.5-x86_64"
    node2.vm.hostname = "node2"
    node2.vm.network "private_network", ip: "192.168.1.30"
    node2.vm.provision "shell", path: "provision_slave.sh"
  end
end
```

The Vagrantfile is defined in Ruby. Without diving too deep into the syntax, we will break down the significance of the lines in the file. You will notice a lot of repetition for the three nodes in this file, which are master, node1, and node2. Notice in the file that we are defining the machine's context using config.vm.define and then using the defined name for the first instance. The name we are going to use is `master`. The three machines have four similar directives: `box`, `hostname`, `network`, and `provision`. Let's see what each of these do.

box	Configures what box the machine will be brought up against. The value here should be the name of an installed box or a shorthand name of a box on HashiCorp's Vagrant Cloud. This is quite similar to Docker Hub for Docker images.
hostname	Configures the hostname that the machine should be assigned.
network	Configures networks on the machine. The `private_ network` value allows you to access the machine using a private IP address (not accessible from the internet). On the master, we also used the `forwarded_port` setting to forward the Jenkins port inside the guest to our host machine. This will allow us to access Jenkins on our browser via `http://localhost 8080`.
provision	Configures provisions on the machine so that software can be automatically installed and configured when the machine is created. We are using a bash script to provision our nodes.

The master provisioning script is as follows:

```
provision_master.sh ✕
1   #!/bin/bash
2   # Install Java
3   sudo yum install java-1.8.0-openjdk -y
4   java -version
5
6   # Install Jenkins
7   sudo wget -O /etc/yum.repos.d/jenkins.repo http://pkg.jenkins-ci.org/redhat/jenkins.repo
8   sudo rpm --import https://jenkins-ci.org/redhat/jenkins-ci.org.key
9   sudo yum install jenkins -y
10
11  # Start Jenkins & ensure Jenkins is started at startup
12  sudo service jenkins start
13  sudo chkconfig jenkins on
14
15  # Disable Firewall To Allow Port Forwarding To Host
16  # THIS IS NOT RECOMMENDED ON ANY OTHER ENVIRONMENT
17  sudo service iptables stop
18  |
```

The script installs Java, which Jenkins depends on, and then installs Jenkins and starts up the Jenkins service. Finally, it disables the firewall on the guest to allow for port forwarding. This should not be done in any production environment. Ideally, you should just allow traffic through port 8080 on your firewall to allow access to Jenkins.

The slave provisioning script is as follows:

```
provision_slave.sh  ✕
1   #!/bin/bash
2   # Install Java
3   sudo yum install java-1.8.0-openjdk -y
4   java -version
5
```

On the slaves, we don't need to do much other than ensure that Java is installed. The same version that's installed on the master should be installed on the slaves.

Stopping the Docker Container

If you have been working with Docker up till this point, you need to make sure that you stop all containers to free up any ports that might be in use, especially port 8080, to allow Vagrant to work. To stop Docker containers from working, follow these steps:

1. First, view the running containers by running `docker ps`.

From the output, we can see that the `jenkinsci/blueocean image` is running with a container ID of `e84cdbec2a0c`.

2. Copy the container ID and pass it to the docker `stop` command as shown:

If we run `docker ps` again, we can see that there is no container running and the ports that were mapped are now freed:

Refer to the complete code at https://bit.ly/2utxZa4 and https://bit.ly/2Jre4xh.

3. To spin up your environment, navigate to the `Lesson6` folder in the repository on your terminal after cloning it to your PC. This is where files such as `Vagrantfile`, `provision_master.sh`, and `provision_slave.sh` are located. Inside this directory, run `vagrant up`:

```
⇒ vagrant up
/opt/vagrant/embedded/gems/gems/vagrant-1.9.4/lib/vagrant/util/platform.rb:25: warning: Insecure world writable dir /u
sr/local in PATH, mode 040777
Bringing machine 'master' up with 'virtualbox' provider...
Bringing machine 'node1' up with 'virtualbox' provider...
Bringing machine 'node2' up with 'virtualbox' provider...
==> master: Importing base box 'nrel/CentOS-6.5-x86_64'...
==> master: Matching MAC address for NAT networking...
==> master: Checking if box 'nrel/CentOS-6.5-x86_64' is up to date...
==> master: There was a problem while downloading the metadata for your box
==> master: to check for updates. This is not an error, since it is usually due
==> master: to temporary network problems. This is just a warning. The problem
==> master: encountered was:
```

The output generated by running `vagrant up` is a lot to capture, but if it displays the first few lines similar to the ones depicted in the preceding screenshot, you are off to a great start. Vagrant will basically pull the defined box image and run the steps outlined in the Vagrantfile that we discussed earlier. This includes assigning hostnames and IP addresses, port forwarding, and finally, running the provisioning scripts. You will also notice that the output is helpful enough.

Let this process run to completion until you get control of your terminal back. The final line of output before you get control of your terminal should look something similar to the following:

```
==> node2:    nss-util.x86_64 0:3.28.4-1.el6_9
==> node2: Complete!
==> node2: openjdk version "1.8.0_171"
==> node2: OpenJDK Runtime Environment (build 1.8.0_171-b10)
==> node2: OpenJDK 64-Bit Server VM (build 25.171-b10, mixed mode)
```

4. To ensure that everything works as expected, run the `vagrant status` command on the same directory:

```
⇒ vagrant status
/opt/vagrant/embedded/gems/gems/vagrant-1.9.4/lib/vagrant/util/platform.rb:25: warning: Insecure world writable dir /u
sr/local in PATH, mode 040777
Current machine states:

master                    running (virtualbox)
node1                     running (virtualbox)
node2                     running (virtualbox)

This environment represents multiple VMs. The VMs are all listed
above with their current state. For more information about a specific
VM, run `vagrant status NAME`.
```

From the output, we can see that our three nodes are running, and these are `master`, `node1`, and `node2`. After verifying that our nodes are running, go to your browser and open the URL `http://localhost:8080`. You should be presented with the Jenkins **Getting Started** page as follows:

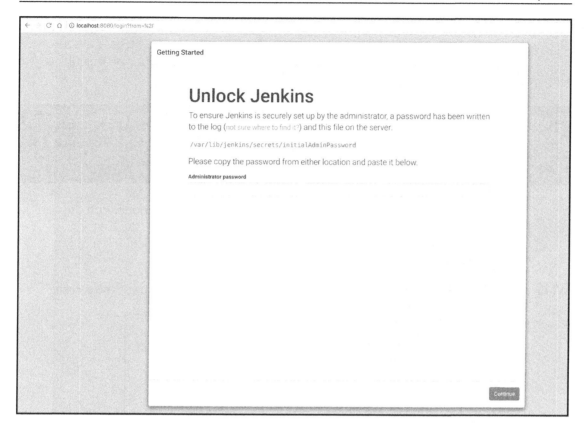

The page requires us to provide the default administrator password. To access this password, we will connect to the master node. On the same directory that you ran the previous vagrant commands, run `vagrant ssh master`. This, as you might have guessed, will connect to the master node:

```
⇒ vagrant ssh master
/opt/vagrant/embedded/gems/gems/vagrant-1.9.4/lib/vagrant/util/platform.rb:25: warning: Insecure world writable dir /u
sr/local in PATH, mode 040777
Welcome to your Vagrant-built virtual machine.
[vagrant@master ~]$
```

This lands us in the terminal of the master node as the default Vagrant user. We want to display the default password in the `/var/lib/jenkins/secrets/initialAdminPassword` file, so run `cat` on this file as `sudo` to display the password:

```
[vagrant@master ~]$ sudo cat /var/lib/jenkins/secrets/initialAdminPassword
366a89d5bdfb4a5fa96399e1ec3a5abb
[vagrant@master ~]$ ▊
```

 Copy this over to the text field on your browser and continue with the setup. The setup process is similar to what we covered in the first chapter; thus it should be familiar to you. Complete the Jenkins setup, create an admin user, and log in to your installation.

While on the dashboard, you will notice something in the lower-left part of the screen:

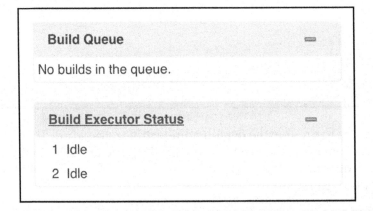

Build Queue

No builds in the queue.

Build Executor Status

1 Idle

2 Idle

 We talked about the build queue and build executors earlier in this section. This is where the status of both of these is displayed. When there is a build running, Jenkins displays on which executor it's running and if there are any builds waiting for the availability of an executor, they are displayed on **Build Queue**.

Verifying Node Connectivity

We are going to verify that our nodes can communicate with each other, first via the ping command and then via SSH. Follow the steps given below to verify node connectivity in Jenkins:

1. Connect to the master node using `vagrant SSH master` and ping both the IP addresses of `node1` and `node2` as follows:

```
[vagrant@master ~]$ ping 192.168.1.20 -c 4
PING 192.168.1.20 (192.168.1.20) 56(84) bytes of data.
64 bytes from 192.168.1.20: icmp_seq=1 ttl=64 time=0.308 ms
64 bytes from 192.168.1.20: icmp_seq=2 ttl=64 time=0.303 ms
64 bytes from 192.168.1.20: icmp_seq=3 ttl=64 time=0.272 ms
64 bytes from 192.168.1.20: icmp_seq=4 ttl=64 time=0.470 ms

--- 192.168.1.20 ping statistics ---
4 packets transmitted, 4 received, 0% packet loss, time 3003ms
rtt min/avg/max/mdev = 0.272/0.338/0.470/0.078 ms
[vagrant@master ~]$ ping 192.168.1.30 -c 4
PING 192.168.1.30 (192.168.1.30) 56(84) bytes of data.
64 bytes from 192.168.1.30: icmp_seq=1 ttl=64 time=0.797 ms
64 bytes from 192.168.1.30: icmp_seq=2 ttl=64 time=0.333 ms
64 bytes from 192.168.1.30: icmp_seq=3 ttl=64 time=0.247 ms
64 bytes from 192.168.1.30: icmp_seq=4 ttl=64 time=0.221 ms

--- 192.168.1.30 ping statistics ---
4 packets transmitted, 4 received, 0% packet loss, time 3001ms
rtt min/avg/max/mdev = 0.221/0.399/0.797/0.234 ms
[vagrant@master ~]$
```

The `-c` flag just specifies to send 4 packets to the nodes. The output shows that the nodes can communicate as there is 0% packet loss.

2. Connect to the two nodes from our master using SSH. Run `ssh vagrant@192.168.1.20` to connect to `node1` as follows:

```
[vagrant@master ~]$ ssh vagrant@192.168.1.20
vagrant@192.168.1.20's password:
Last login: Sat May  5 16:26:40 2018 from 192.168.1.10
Welcome to your Vagrant-built virtual machine.
[vagrant@node1 ~]$
```

3. Enter `yes` if a prompt asking you about the authenticity of the host is displayed and use `vagrant` as the password.
4. Note that, as you type in the password, it will not be displayed.

 When Vagrant provisions VMs, you do not want to specify any SSH settings. You can find out more at `https://www.vagrantup.com/docs/vagrantfile/ssh_settings.html`. This will create a user with the username `vagrant` and password `vagrant` by default. We will use this default user to access both our nodes since we did not specify any users in our Vagrantfile.

5. Repeat this process to connect to `node2`. You can do this from either the `master` or `node2`. Note The connection will work as long as you provide the correct credentials, since all nodes are on the same network.

With that, you have successfully verified that the nodes can communicate with each other; thus, the next steps we will take in this chapter should work without any problems.

Securely Connecting to the Slaves

In the previous section, we provisioned our environment with a master that has Jenkins installed on it, and also added two nodes to our network. We are going to connect to our nodes via SSH with a process similar to what we did in the previous section when verifying connectivity, but this time via the Jenkins user interface.

Adding Slave Nodes

Currently, on our Jenkins setup, there is only one node and that is the master with two build executors, as we mentioned earlier. From the main dashboard, we can verify this by navigating to **Manage Jenkins -> Manage Nodes**:

We can see that there is only one node, which is the `master`. This label is assigned by default to the node on which Jenkins is installed. Now, let's add a slave node `node1` using the following steps:

1. On the left-hand side of the same view, we can see **New Node** on the menu.
2. Click on this and you will be presented with the following view:

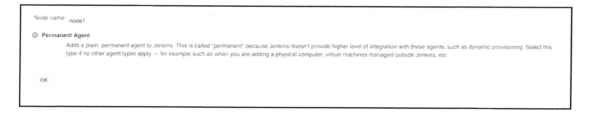

3. Configure the preceding form and press **OK**. You will then be presented with the following view for further configuration of the node:

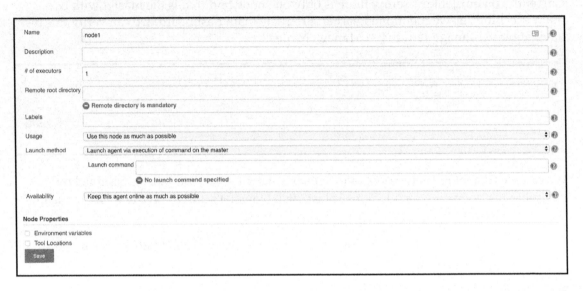

4. For the configuration, fill in the first six form fields as follows:
    - **Name**: node1
    - **Description**: Our First Node (optional)
    - **# of executors**: 2
    - **Remote root directory**: /tmp/
    - **Labels**: node1
    - **Usage**: Use this node as much as possible

5. For the **Launch method**, select the drop-down and choose **Launch slave agents via SSH**. This will present us with another form, as follows:

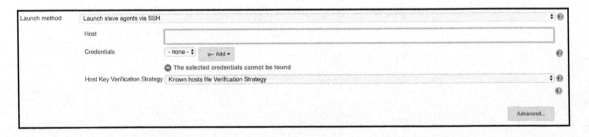

For the host, enter the IP address as `node1`, as defined in the `Vagrantfile`: `192.168.1.20`. We will then create credentials to allow our master to connect to `node1`. Click on the **Add** drop-down next to the credentials field and select **Jenkins**.

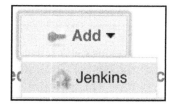

This will display a form, which we will configure. For the password field, enter `vagrant` (these are the same SSH credentials we used earlier when verifying host connectivity):

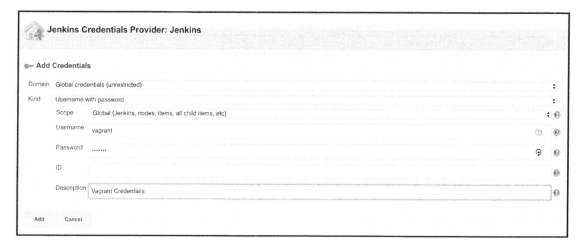

6. Click **Add** and select the credentials you just created on the previous view:

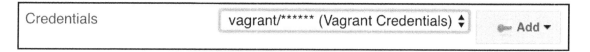

7. For the **Host Key Verification Strategy**, we are going to select **Non verifying Verification Strategy**, as follows:

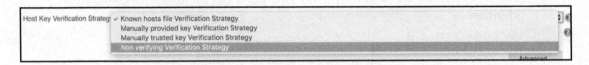

 Remember that when connecting via SSH on the terminal, you are prompted to verify that the host is authentic, especially if you haven't connected to the host before. This will prevent the connection from failing and reduces the administrative tasks we have to perform if we want to verify our hosts. This is not recommended on production environments. Always ensure that you verify the hosts you are connecting to.

8. Finally, for **Availability**, select **Keep this agent online as much as possible**, as follows:

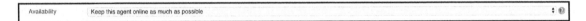

9. Finally, press **Save** to add the node. Wait a few seconds and your node will go online if you configured everything correctly:

S	Name ↓	Architecture	Clock Difference	Free Disk Space	Free Swap Space	Free Temp Space	Response Time
	master	Linux (amd64)	In sync	181.07 GB	3.97 GB	181.07 GB	0ms
	node1	Linux (amd64)	In sync	181.07 GB	3.97 GB	181.07 GB	2733ms
	Data obtained	2 sec	1.8 sec	1.6 sec	1.5 sec	1.6 sec	1.6 sec

Refresh status

10. If your node does not go online, click on the drop-down on the node name and select **Log**, as follows:

This will show you the connection attempt logs, and if anything goes wrong, you will be able to find out from this view:

```
DIRSTACK=()
EUID=500
GROUPS=()
G_BROKEN_FILENAMES=1
HOME=/home/vagrant
HOSTNAME=master
HOSTTYPE=x86_64
IFS=$' \t\n'
LANG=en_US.UTF-8
LESSOPEN='|/usr/bin/lesspipe.sh %s'
LOGNAME=vagrant
MACHTYPE=x86_64-redhat-linux-gnu
MAIL=/var/mail/vagrant
OPTERR=1
OPTIND=1
OSTYPE=linux-gnu
PATH=/usr/local/bin:/bin:/usr/bin
PIPESTATUS=([0]="0")
PPID=4009
PS4='+ '
PWD=/home/vagrant
SHELL=/bin/bash
SHELLOPTS=braceexpand:hashall:interactive-comments
SHLVL=1
SSH_CLIENT='127.0.0.1 43955 22'
SSH_CONNECTION='127.0.0.1 43955 127.0.0.1 22'
TERM=dumb
UID=500
USER=vagrant
_=/etc/bashrc
[05/05/18 17:51:53] [SSH] Checking java version of java
[05/05/18 17:51:54] [SSH] java -version returned 1.8.0_171.
[05/05/18 17:51:54] [SSH] Starting sftp client.
[05/05/18 17:51:54] [SSH] Copying latest slave.jar...
[05/05/18 17:51:54] [SSH] Copied 770,802 bytes.
Expanded the channel window size to 4MB
[05/05/18 17:51:54] [SSH] Starting slave process: cd "/tmp" && java  -jar slave.jar
<===[JENKINS REMOTING CAPACITY]===>channel started
Remoting version: 3.20
This is a Unix agent
Evacuated stdout
Agent successfully connected and online
```

11. Under the **Build Executor Status** section, we can see that we now have two nodes (`master` and `node1`) and four build executors in total:

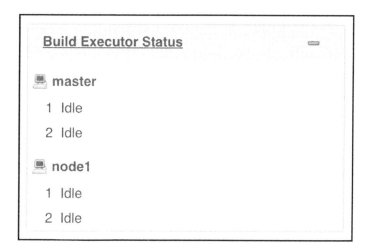

Activity: Adding Slave Nodes in Jenkins

Scenario

Over the past few days, developers in your company have been complaining about slow build times. Upon further investigation, you noticed a lot of builds queued, waiting for an available executor on your current nodes. You have also noticed that CPU and memory usage is high from your monitoring; thus, you have been tasked with adding another slave node to your setup (we will be using `node2` from the Vagrant setup we have been using in this chapter).

Aim

To get you conversant with setting up Jenkins slave nodes

Prerequisites

Ensure the following:

- You have Jenkins up and running
- You are logged in as the **Administrator**
- You have followed through this chapter and have provisioned the Vagrant hosts, which are `master`, `node1`, and `node2`

Steps for Completion

1. On the Jenkins dashboard, go to **Manage Jenkins** -> **Manage Nodes**. On the left-hand side menu, select **New Node**.

2. Enter `node2` as the node name and select **Permanent Agent**.

3. For the node's configuration, use the same configuration as you did for `node1` earlier in this section, aside for the points outlined as follows:
   - **Name**: `node2`
   - **Description**: <enter a different description for this node>
   - **Labels**: `node2`
   - **Usage**: Only build jobs with label expressions matching these nodes

4. Configure the node to be launched via SSH and use the same credentials you used for `node1`, which are the Vagrant credentials.

5. Save the configuration and check the agent's logs to ensure that it has successfully connected to your master.

6. The output log should look like the following if you have successfully set up node2:

```
[05/05/18 19:22:33] [SSH] Checking java version of java
[05/05/18 19:22:33] [SSH] java -version returned 1.8.0_171.
[05/05/18 19:22:33] [SSH] Starting sftp client.
[05/05/18 19:22:33] [SSH] Copying latest slave.jar...
[05/05/18 19:22:33] [SSH] Copied 770,802 bytes.
Expanded the channel window size to 4MB
[05/05/18 19:22:33] [SSH] Starting slave process: cd "/tmp" && java  -jar slave.jar
<===[JENKINS REMOTING CAPACITY]===>channel started
Remoting version: 3.20
This is a Unix agent
Evacuated stdout
Agent successfully connected and online
```

Configuring Tasks to Run on our Slaves

While configuring our nodes, you noticed one setting that involved how and when we want our nodes to be used, and this was under the **Usage** setting. We can set it to either of the following:

- **Use this node as much as possible**
- **Only build jobs with label expressions matching this node**

The second option offers some restrictions on which tasks can be run on a node. This is useful for cases where you have a custom node to perform certain tasks, for example, performance testing, and you don't want other tasks to interfere with this. In the final exercise of the previous section, we added a node to our Jenkins setup, node2, and specified its usage as **Only build jobs with label expressions matching these nodes**. This node will be idle unless we create projects and instruct them to only run on node2. In this section, we will learn how to configure a freestyle project to run on a specific node.

Running Freestyle Projects on a Node

Let us see how we can run freestyle projects on node2. Follow these steps:

1. On the Jenkins dashboard, select **New Item**, select **Freestyle Project**, and press **OK** to create the project.

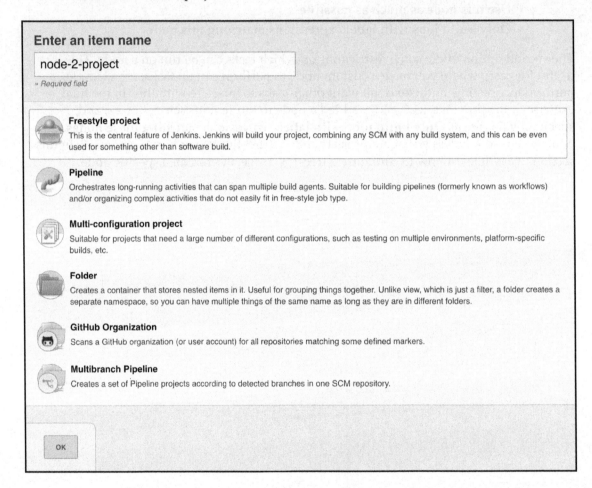

2. Under the **General** tab, enter a project description (optional), select **Restrict where this project can be run**, and enter `node2` in the text field. You will notice that Jenkins autocompletes with the available nodes.

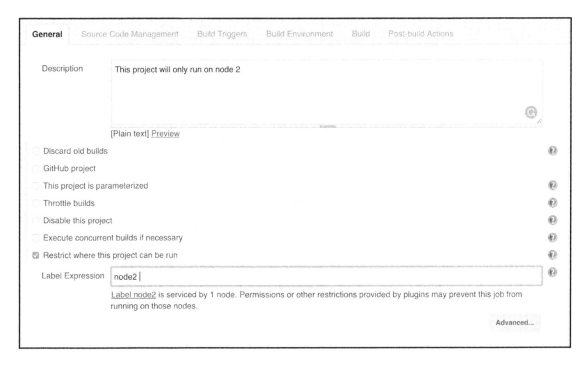

3. Add a build step that will execute a shell command, as follows:

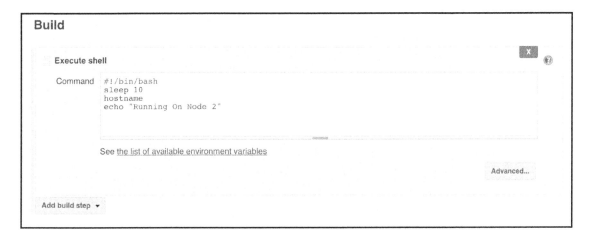

4. Select **Apply** and **Save** to persist your changes. We are going to run the project from the main Jenkins dashboard as opposed to the project dashboard so that we can watch our executors.

5. Click on the drop-down on the project name and select **Build Now**, as shown:

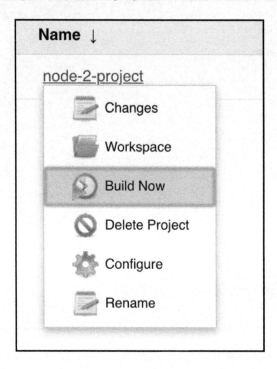

If we watch the executors at the bottom left, we can see that our project is running on `node2`, as we defined in the configuration:

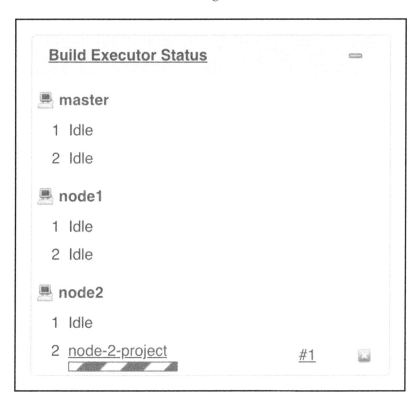

6. Digging deeper into the build, we can see the following from the **Console Output**:

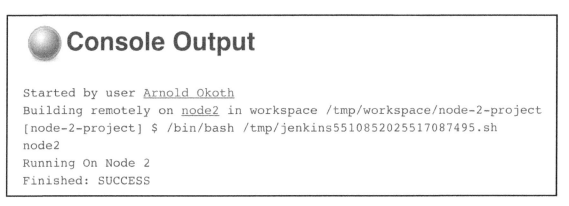

The `hostname` command will display exactly that, the hostname of the node, which in our case is `node2`. We used the sleep command to give us enough time to view the build running on the executor, otherwise it would have disappeared very fast since our build step does not do much and will complete after a very short time.

Running Pipelines on Different Nodes

When working with pipelines, we can assign different stages to different nodes. Recall the node directive that we covered in the previous chapter. The node directive defines where to run the rest of the pipeline directives enclosed in its scope. For example, the pipeline we defined in the previous chapter is as follows:

```
1  node('master') {
2      printMessage('Running Pipeline')
3
4      stage("Fetch Source Code") {
5          git 'https://github.com/arnoldokoth/lesson5'
6      }
7
8      stage("Testing") {
9          sh 'python test_functions.py'
10     }
11
12     printMessage('Pipeline Complete')
13 }
14
15 def printMessage(message) {
16     echo "${message}"
17 }
18
```

This pipeline will be run on the master node. When left blank, the pipeline will be run on the master by default or any other node that the master is freely allowed to use. In this section, we will create a basic pipeline and configure it to run on different nodes.

1. On the Jenkins dashboard, create a **New project**, select **Pipeline** as the project type, and select **OK** to create the project:

2. Add the optional project description and scroll the pipeline section. We will be adding the following pipeline script to the project, which is provided in the code files for this chapter.

```
Jenkinsfile ✕
1    node {
2        stage("Might Run On Node 1 Or Master") {
3            printMessage("Running")
4            sh 'sleep 10'
5            sh 'hostname'
6        }
7    }
8
9    node('node2') {
10       stage("On Node 2") {
11           printMessage("Running On Node 2")
12           sh 'sleep 10'
13           sh 'hostname'
14       }
15   }
16
17   def printMessage(message) {
18       echo "${message}"
19   }
20
```

Refer to the complete code, which has been placed at https://bit.ly/ 2Njw5jh.

3. Copy and paste the contents of the file to the pipeline script text area. The final configuration should look as follows:

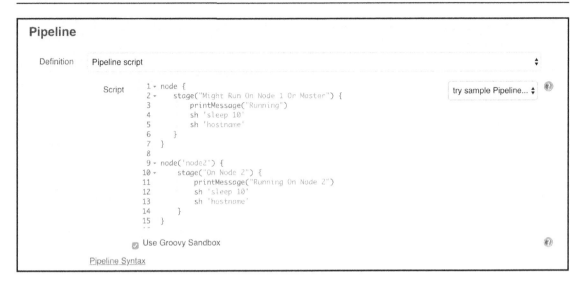

4. Press **Apply** and **Save** to persist your configuration. On the project dashboard, select **Build Now** and click on the current build's **Console Output** as shown:

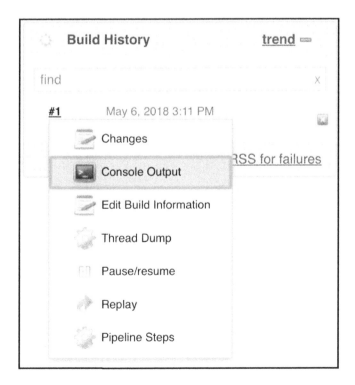

The console output for our build is as follows, and we can see that our pipeline ran on different nodes:

```
[Pipeline] node
Running on Jenkins in /var/lib/jenkins/workspace/node-pipeline
[Pipeline] {
[Pipeline] stage
[Pipeline] { (Might Run On Node 1 Or Master)
[Pipeline] echo
Running
[Pipeline] sh
[node-pipeline] Running shell script
+ sleep 10
[Pipeline] sh
[node-pipeline] Running shell script
+ hostname
master
[Pipeline] }
[Pipeline] // stage
[Pipeline] }
[Pipeline] // node
[Pipeline] node
Running on node2 in /tmp/workspace/node-pipeline
[Pipeline] {
[Pipeline] stage
[Pipeline] { (On Node 2)
[Pipeline] echo
Running On Node 2
[Pipeline] sh
[node-pipeline] Running shell script
+ sleep 10
[Pipeline] sh
[node-pipeline] Running shell script
+ hostname
node2
[Pipeline] }
[Pipeline] // stage
[Pipeline] }
[Pipeline] // node
[Pipeline] End of Pipeline
Finished: SUCCESS
```

Spinning Down the Vagrant Environment

In this section, we will spin up a new Vagrant environment; thus, we need to destroy our previous setup. We must first check the status of our environment by running the `vagrant status` command:

```
→ Lesson6 git:(master) ✗ vagrant status
Current machine states:

master                    running (virtualbox)
node1                     running (virtualbox)
node2                     running (virtualbox)

This environment represents multiple VMs. The VMs are all listed
above with their current state. For more information about a specific
VM, run `vagrant status NAME`.
→ Lesson6 git:(master) ✗ █
```

From the output, we can see that we have three boxes running.

To spin down the Vagrant environment, follow these steps:

1. Run `vagrant destroy` and enter `y` on the following prompts:

```
→ Lesson6 git:(master) ✗ vagrant destroy
    node2: Are you sure you want to destroy the 'node2' VM? [y/N] y
==> node2: Forcing shutdown of VM...
==> node2: Destroying VM and associated drives...
    node1: Are you sure you want to destroy the 'node1' VM? [y/N] y
==> node1: Forcing shutdown of VM...
==> node1: Destroying VM and associated drives...
    master: Are you sure you want to destroy the 'master' VM? [y/N] y
==> master: Forcing shutdown of VM...
==> master: Destroying VM and associated drives...
→ Lesson6 git:(master) ✗ █
```

2. Run `vagrant status` to verify that the virtual machines are no longer running and that they are in the `not created` state:

```
➜  Lesson6 git:(master) ✗ vagrant status
Current machine states:

master                    not created (virtualbox)
node1                     not created (virtualbox)
node2                     not created (virtualbox)

This environment represents multiple VMs. The VMs are all listed
above with their current state. For more information about a specific
VM, run `vagrant status NAME`.
➜  Lesson6 git:(master) ✗ 
```

Activity: Bringing it all Together

Scenario

You have been tasked with setting up a two-node build environment with a master and one agent. The master will have one executor and the agent will have two executors. After this, you have been tasked with creating a view for the Code Hive project that will house build tasks for the project. You will then create a demo pipeline that will run on the agent to verify that the setup works as expected and that the agent can build the project as required.

Aim

To create a demo pipeline with a two-node build environment with a master and one agent

Prerequisites

Make sure you have done the following:

1. Referred to the complete code at `https://bit.ly/2NXAKJ4`, `https://bit.ly/2NVoc19`, and `https://bit.ly/2zPuIH8`.
2. Created a GitHub account

Steps for Completion

1. Using the provided code files, spin up this environment. You can either clone the whole repository and change directories to the `Lesson6/ActivityA` folder or create your own directory and add the files into it.

2. Inside the folder containing the `Vagrantfile`, `master.sh`, and `agent.sh` scripts, run the vagrant up command. This will begin the provisioning process for both your nodes. The final output for this command is as follows:

```
==> agent1:    nss-util.x86_64 0:3.28.4-1.el6_9
==> agent1: Complete!
==> agent1: openjdk version "1.8.0_171"
==> agent1: OpenJDK Runtime Environment (build 1.8.0_171-b10)
==> agent1: OpenJDK 64-Bit Server VM (build 25.171-b10, mixed mode)
```

3. Open your browser and navigate to the URL `http://localhost:8080`.

4. To unlock Jenkins, use `vagrant ssh` to connect to the master and use the following command to reveal the password:

```
[vagrant@master ~]$ sudo cat /var/lib/jenkins/secrets/initialAdminPassword
1dbcf0f84ea04316af5982ac378bbd4d
[vagrant@master ~]$
```

5. Complete the Jenkins setup by installing the recommended plugins and creating the administrator user.

6. We will first add our agent to our build environment. From the dashboard, navigate to **Manage Jenkins** -> **Manage Nodes**. From the menu on the left, select **New Node**. Configure the node as follows:

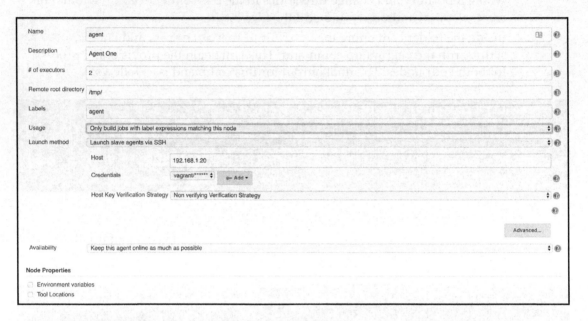

7. For the SSH authentication, create a username with a **password** credential type with the username `vagrant` and the password `vagrant`.

8. After completing this, select Save and, back on the agent dashboard, select Refresh Status until the agent comes online:

Currently, the master has two build executors, but remember that we were tasked with configuring the master to only have one. From the dashboard, navigate to **Manage Jenkins** -> **Configure System** and change the number of executors to one.

9. Select **Apply** and **Save**:

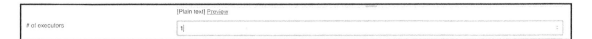

10. On the Jenkins dashboard, navigate to **My Views** -> **New View** to create the **Code Hive** project view. We are going to create our demo project under this view:

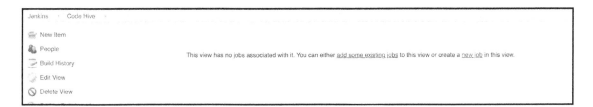

11. Click on the hyperlink to **New Job** to create the new job.

12. Configure the new pipeline project as shown and give the project an appropriate name, ensuring that the checkbox next to the **OK** button is selected:

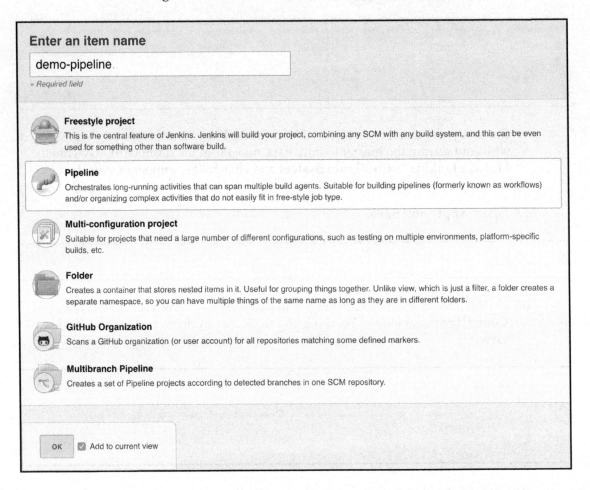

Enter an item name

demo-pipeline.

» *Required field*

Freestyle project
This is the central feature of Jenkins. Jenkins will build your project, combining any SCM with any build system, and this can be even used for something other than software build.

Pipeline
Orchestrates long-running activities that can span multiple build agents. Suitable for building pipelines (formerly known as workflows) and/or organizing complex activities that do not easily fit in free-style job type.

Multi-configuration project
Suitable for projects that need a large number of different configurations, such as testing on multiple environments, platform-specific builds, etc.

Folder
Creates a container that stores nested items in it. Useful for grouping things together. Unlike view, which is just a filter, a folder creates a separate namespace, so you can have multiple things of the same name as long as they are in different folders.

GitHub Organization
Scans a GitHub organization (or user account) for all repositories matching some defined markers.

Multibranch Pipeline
Creates a set of Pipeline projects according to detected branches in one SCM repository.

OK ☑ Add to current view

13. In the pipeline configuration section of the project, add the following script, which is provided in the code files:

```
Jenkinsfile ✕
 1    node {
 2        stage("Testing Stage") {
 3            printMessage("Running Testing Stage")
 4            sh 'hostname'
 5        }
 6    }
 7
 8    node('agent') {
 9        stage("Testing Stage: Agent") {
10            printMessage("Running Testing Stage On Agent")
11            sh 'hostname'
12        }
13    }
14
15    def printMessage(message){
16        echo "${message}"
17    }
18
```

14. Configure the project as shown and select **Save**:

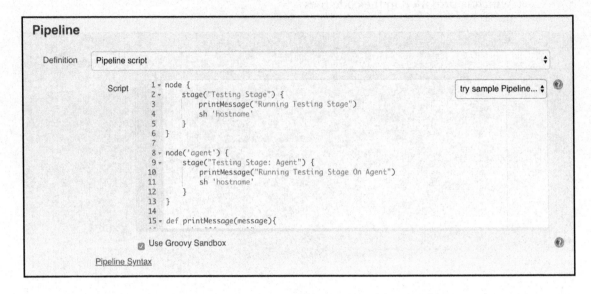

15. On the project dashboard, select **Build Now**. The console output is as follows:

```
Running on Jenkins in /var/lib/jenkins/workspace/demo-pipeline
[Pipeline] {
[Pipeline] stage
[Pipeline] { (Testing Stage)
[Pipeline] echo
Running Testing Stage
[Pipeline] sh
[demo-pipeline] Running shell script
+ hostname
master
[Pipeline] }
[Pipeline] // stage
[Pipeline] }
[Pipeline] // node
[Pipeline] node
Running on agent in /tmp/workspace/demo-pipeline
[Pipeline] {
[Pipeline] stage
[Pipeline] { (Testing Stage: Agent)
[Pipeline] echo
Running Testing Stage On Agent
[Pipeline] sh
[demo-pipeline] Running shell script
+ hostname
agent1
[Pipeline] }
[Pipeline] // stage
[Pipeline] }
[Pipeline] // node
[Pipeline] End of Pipeline
Finished: SUCCESS
```

From the output, notice that both our nodes can run our builds and are working as expected.

Summary

In this chapter, we have learned how to set up agents on Jenkins to run our builds. We then learned the advantages of distributed builds and how they help extend our build environment. Lastly, we learned how to run freestyle and pipeline projects on our agents. Well done! We've come to the end of our book on Jenkins. Now, you can implement the concepts learned in your work environment for real.

Other Books You May Enjoy

If you enjoyed this book, you may be interested in these other books by Packt:

Hands-On Data Science and Python Machine Learning
Frank Kane

ISBN: 978-1-78728-074-8

- Learn how to clean your data and ready it for analysis
- Implement the popular clustering and regression methods in Python
- Train efficient machine learning models using decision trees and random forests
- Visualize the results of your analysis using Python's Matplotlib library
- Use Apache Spark's MLlib package to perform machine learning on large datasets

Kali Linux Cookbook - Second Edition
Corey P. Schultz, Bob Perciaccante

ISBN: 978-1-78439-030-3

- Acquire the key skills of ethical hacking to perform penetration testing
- Learn how to perform network reconnaissance
- Discover vulnerabilities in hosts
- Attack vulnerabilities to take control of workstations and servers
- Understand password cracking to bypass security
- Learn how to hack into wireless networks
- Attack web and database servers to exfiltrate data
- Obfuscate your command and control connections to avoid firewall and IPS detection

Leave a review - let other readers know what you think

Please share your thoughts on this book with others by leaving a review on the site that you bought it from. If you purchased the book from Amazon, please leave us an honest review on this book's Amazon page. This is vital so that other potential readers can see and use your unbiased opinion to make purchasing decisions, we can understand what our customers think about our products, and our authors can see your feedback on the title that they have worked with Packt to create. It will only take a few minutes of your time, but is valuable to other potential customers, our authors, and Packt. Thank you!

Index

P

parameterized projects
  creating 93, 95, 96, 97
  parameters, accessing 109, 113, 114, 115, 116, 118
  setting up 109, 111
parameters
  configuring, for projects 92
pipeline
  about 137
  creating 154, 158, 171, 174, 175, 176, 177
plugin management
  about 29, 30, 31, 32
  activity 40, 41, 42
  usage principles 32
plugins
  Administration plugins 33
  Build Management 34
  Source Code Management (SCM) plugins 33
  User Interface (UI) plugins 33
Post-Build Actions 69
pull requests
  building, Jenkins used 170

R

repository
  setting up 140, 143, 144, 146, 148, 149

S

sample plugin
  installing for InternetMeme 36, 37, 38, 39
scripted pipeline
  about 153

def directive 153
dir directive 153
git directive 153
node directive 153
sh directive 153
stage directive 153
security
  about 23
  legacy mode 24
  Matrix-based security 24
  project-based Matrix authorization strategy 24
SSH Server 57
SSL Certificates 56
stable release 47
string parameters
  accessing 99, 102, 103, 105, 107, 108
  creating 99, 100

U

upstream projects
  configuring 123, 124, 126
  creating 119, 120, 121
  running 126, 128
User Interface (UI) plugins
  about 33
user management
  about 23
  analyzing 23
  Matrix-based security 24

V

variable
  about 161

Made in the USA
Columbia, SC
02 December 2019